Erotic
Justice

Erotic
Justice

A Liberating Ethic of Sexuality

MARVIN M. ELLISON

Westminster John Knox Press
Louisville, Kentucky

Book design by Jennifer K. Cox
Cover design by Kim Wohlenhaus
Cover illustration © Phototake, David Gnizak, PNI.

First edition

Published by Westminster John Knox Press
Louisville, Kentucky

This book is printed on acid-free paper that meets the American National Standards Institute Z39.48 standard. ♾

PRINTED IN THE UNITED STATES OF AMERICA

96 97 98 99 00 01 02 03 04 05 — 10 9 8 7 6 5 4 3 2 1

Library of Congress Cataloging-in-Publication Data

Ellison, Marvin M.
    Erotic justice : a liberating ethic of sexuality / Marvin M. Ellison — 1st ed.
        p.   cm.
    Includes index:
    ISBN 0-664-25646-5 (alk. paper)
    1. Sexual ethics. 2. Social ethics. 3. Sex—Religious aspects—Christianity.
    4. Homosexuality—Religious aspects—Christianity. 5. Liberation theology. I. Title.
    HQ32.E566 1996
    306.7—dc20

                                                                                96-16031

For

Beverly Rankin Ellison
beloved daughter

and

Beverly Wildung Harrison
beloved mentor

passionate lovers of justice

Re-examine all you have been told at school or church or in any book, dismiss whatever insults your own soul, and your very flesh shall be a great poem . . . in every motion and joint of your body.

—Walt Whitman, *Leaves of Grass*
Preface to the 1855 edition

Contents

Acknowledgments

This book carries forward work I first developed for the Presbyterian Church (U.S.A.) by coauthoring a 1991 study document, *Keeping Body and Soul Together: Sexuality, Spirituality, and Social Justice*. I am grateful to John C. Carey, chair of the task force, and to Thelma Burgonio-Watson, Janet Fishburn, Grace Kim, Daniel Smith, and Sylvia Thorson Smith for encouraging my work then and now.

Some material contained in these pages received the kind of constructive feedback that every author longs for, through public presentations for the Sexuality Interest Group of the Society of Christian Ethics, at the West Hollywood Presbyterian Church; the Episcopal Diocese of Rhode Island; Grinnell College and the First Presbyterian Church of Grinnell, Iowa; Plymouth Congregational Church, Des Moines; Ghost Ranch Conference Center; the University of Maine at Orono; and workshops sponsored by Planned Parenthood of Northern New England.

At earlier stages of research and writing, I received financial assistance through the Association of Theological Schools' Younger Scholars program and from the American Academy of Religion's Research Assistance Grant program. I am grateful also to the Trustees of Bangor Theological Seminary for making a sabbatical leave possible, to President Malcolm Warford and Dean Glenn Miller for their ongoing support, and to the many seminary students who, over the years, have encouraged me to teach my passion.

Along the way, Frank Brooks, Susan Davies, Celeste DeRoche, Michael Dwinell, Gail Geisenhainer, Anne Gilson, Robin Gorsline, and Sylvia Thorson Smith read portions of this manuscript and engaged me in wonderful conversations. Social ethicists Elly Haney, Beverly Harrison, and Mary Hobgood, along with legal scholar Anne Underwood, generously made their time available to read the manuscript in its entirety. Because of their enthusiasm for this project and their suggestions for revision, I have been longer at this task than I had bargained for, but their insights have helped produce a better book. I am blessed by their friendship and what they teach about the pain and glory of loving justice. Stephanie Egnotovich and Nancy Roseberry at Westminster John Knox have generously shared their expertise at all the right moments. I appreciate their professionalism, as well as their personal determination to make critical resources available, for church and society, on controversial topics.

I am especially grateful for, and humbled by, Beverly Ellison's patient support and loving care throughout the weeks and months required to complete this project. She must know far, far better than I why justice, unlike charity, must begin at home.

Grateful acknowledgment is made to the following for permission to reprint copyrighted material.

Church and Society, for Marvin M. Ellison, "Sexuality and Spirituality: An Intimate—and Intimidating—Connection," vol. 80, no. 2 (November-December 1989).

International Creative Management, Inc., for portions of *Beloved*, by Toni Morrison, © 1987 by Toni Morrison, published by Alfred A. Knopf, Inc. Permission granted by International Creative Management, Inc.

The Pilgrim Press, for Marvin M. Ellison, "Refusing to be 'Good Soldiers': An Agenda for Men," in *Redefining Sexual Ethics: A Sourcebook of Essays, Stories, and Poems*, ed. Susan E. Davies and Eleanor H. Haney, published by The Pilgrim Press, 1991.

Presbyterian Church (U.S.A.), Office of the General Assembly, for Marvin M. Ellison, "Framework," in *Keeping Body and Soul Together: Sexuality, Spirituality, and Social Justice*, 1991 (reprinted as *Presbyterians and Human Sexuality*, 1991).

Introduction
Needed: Liberating Moral Discourse on Sexuality

We must be prophets of
a sex positive truth.[1]

—Larry J. Uhrig

Everywhere in this culture people realize that sexuality and family life are in crisis, but no consensus exists about the nature of the problem or its solution. Moreover, few associate their personal troubles with social injustice, and yet this link must be forged if people are to make sense of their lives and find ways to be genuinely at home in their bodies and in the shared body politic. The bad news, in evidence everywhere, is that human sexuality is distorted by various forms of social oppression. The good news, less evident but critically important, is that people have a place immediately accessible to them—their own body space, as well as their intimate connections with others—within which to mount resistance to injustice and also experiment with freedom.

Conventional moral discourse, in both its liberal and conservative guises, obscures matters by misidentifying the source of the problem as sexuality itself. The tendency is either to locate the problem in individual pathology or to privatize sexuality within a supposedly nonconflictual sphere of interpersonal intimacy. Instead, we need an alternative discourse that understands the political, as well as the personal, dimensions of this crisis. The crisis in sexuality is properly located in the eroticizing of dominant/subordinate social relations and in the distortion of love by racism, sexism, and other injustices. Sexuality and the quality of personal life are dialectically related to the wider social order. All aspects of human life, including eroticism, are shaped by power relations, specifically gender inequities, race supremacy, classism, and cultural elitism. A constructive social ethic of sexuality must keep this personal-structural connection in focus.

The starting point for ethical inquiry about sexuality should be the defining fact of our social world: We live in a world broken and alienated

1

by multiple forms of oppression. Structural injustices shape—and mis-shape—our self-understanding, including our self-awareness as sexual persons. Injustice, I argue in this book, distorts the humanly good desire for intimate connection and remolds it as a perverted desire for possession and control. We need moral discourse that can confront the depth of this cultural crisis and also appreciate how justice, as communally secured respect and regard for persons, is foundational to good loving. There is a message here of hope. Our loving well requires that we pursue justice in all social relations, including those closest to our skin. Justice and love are tightly intertwined soul mates.

Sexuality, as I define it here, includes genital sex but refers more broadly to our embodied capacity for intimate connection. Erotic desire seeks physical, emotional, and spiritual embrace of others, the world, and God, the sacred Source of life. By *justice* I refer to the ongoing, never-ending journey to remake community by strengthening relationship. Justice-making attends to how people's well-being is enhanced or diminished by prevailing patterns of social power and powerlessness. A commitment to justice means correcting whatever harms people, other earth creatures, and the earth itself.

A justice-centered sexual ethic is grounded in a theological vision of an inclusive, participatory social order with several characteristics: Power is fairly distributed and used to build community, goods and resources are equitably produced and shared, and people thrive because they are deeply valued, cared for, and respected in all their diversity. *Sexual justice* honors sexual well-being as a significant dimension of the good of persons. A just society fosters the moral right of all persons, without distinction, to love and be loved and to freely express their desire for intimate, respectful connection.

We need intelligent, compassionate, and morally astute reflection about human sexuality that stays in touch with real people's struggles (and triumphs) in a complex, often daunting world. We need discourse that is comfortable with human differences and moral diversity. We need an ethic in tune with how most people, most of the time, strive to do their best under less than optimal circumstances. We need, but do not yet have, a Christian sexual ethic that takes seriously our personal desire for respect and care, but also empowers us to reorder our communities toward greater inclusivity and shared well-being.

A genuinely liberating ethic is unabashedly passionate. The longing for dignity and purpose in our life pursuits can arouse, deep within us, an abiding sense of the goodness of life, an attentiveness to joy and suffering, and an urgency about protecting persons and communities from harm. This kind of strong, full-bodied passion longs to share life's struggles and pleasures generously with others. Soul-satisfying pleasure is found in pursuing justice as right-relatedness in all our connections, from the most intimate to the most public. Making justice real, in the large and small places of our lives, can both excite people and demand that they work for a radically different world. In short, we need a liberating Christian ethic of sexuality that turns people on to justice, in their bedrooms and beyond.

Many of us hunger for such a liberating ethic and the life it seeks to generate. We struggle to sort out the ethical implications of issues ranging from reproductive technologies to changing gender roles, from inclusive language to domestic violence, from AIDS and other sexually transmitted diseases to nonauthoritarian relational and family patterns. As a gay man, I include myself among those struggling with these and other issues and also yearning passionately for greater justice and for the respect due me and all other people. Because I am also a single parent of a teenaged daughter, I struggle with how to make the world, and immediately my own home and city, safer for her and other women and children. As a Christian ethicist, I am deeply disturbed by the escalating suffering of people in this country and across the globe, but I am equally troubled by widespread social passivity and especially by the absence of courageous, organized leadership within progressive religious communities. In this book, I explore how this apathy is linked to the cultural crisis in sexuality. Reclaiming an erotic sense of justice is an often-overlooked avenue for mobilizing people's energies for both personal and social transformation. Part of the moral wisdom emerging from feminist and gay liberation movements is that we are not likely to have either personal or social transformation without the other.

As a social ethicist, I find myself most in sync with progressive people of all genders, classes, and colors who, like myself, have committed their life energy to confronting oppression, developing more humane community, and protecting the earth. All forms of oppression, including sexual oppression, violate the earth and/or people's bodies, offend the human spirit, and block authentic community. Advocacy for sexual justice, far from being a trivial matter in this world of multiple injustices, sparks a politically radicalizing desire in people, mediated in and through their bodies, for self-respect and freedom. When, as I shall argue later, sexuality is repressed and people are cut off from their feelings or when domination is eroticized as sexy and titillating, people are denied an inner resource that otherwise might energize them to resist abuse and demand fairer treatment.

My social location as a gay man, parent, and educator-activist shapes my moral vision, but because I have both access to social power and some measure of social powerlessness as a member of a sexual minority, matters are more complex. My white skin, middle-class status, and professional employment protect me from the effects of various social injustices that bear down, with much greater force, on those without such assets and resources. In a culture of radical individualism, I and others like me might well succumb to the false belief that each of us can somehow "rise above" it all and "make it" entirely on our own. However, the most reliable way I know for keeping honest about my own need for significant personal, as well as sociocultural, change is to stay actively engaged in intersecting social justice movements, including movements to end racism, sexism, economic exploitation, and ecological destruction. By working with and learning from others whose life struggles differ from my own, I am confronted by the limitations of my own perspective. That confrontation can be painful at times, but also freeing. Self-criticism and ongoing accountability, especially to the disenfranchised, make common cause possible with people who experience other kinds and greater degrees of social vulnerability. Establishing common bonds between us depends not on our having the same social identity but rather on our sharing a common moral commitment to remake communities so that all are welcome, none is excluded, and the earth's integrity is enhanced.

My engagement with others, over a sustained period of time, in education and action for communal transformation has taught me the joys of a kind of justice-making that demands something *for* me, as well as something *of* me. My participation in political alliances now depends on whether gay, lesbian, bisexual, and transgender people are honored as colleagues and mentors in a common struggle. As sexual minorities, our commitments to justice obligate us to say or do nothing that would undermine our own self-respect and well-being. Moreover, we maintain credibility with others as trustworthy allies only by working with equal enthusiasm to dismantle sexism, racism, and class oppression *as part and parcel* of dismantling heterosexism, the primary structure of gay oppression. Our integrity depends on maintaining a complex, multidimensional focus on justice as communal right-relatedness.

I have written this book in the hope of attracting more allies to pursue a broad multicultural justice agenda. The audience I have in mind certainly includes other gay, lesbian, bisexual, and transgender persons, but also feminists of all colors, progressive people on the fringes and in the mainstream of religious communities, and all who are tired of the old sex-negativities and who long for more egalitarian relationships. Our common ground is our yearning for a radical transformation in how sexuality and other social relations are organized in this culture. I also have in mind people who are fed up with Christian myopia about matters of sexuality but who may need a reminder about the roots of that myopia. They may also need reasons to believe that a revitalized Christian tradition may be relevant once again for getting to a better world. Sustaining a desire for justice depends on enlarging our passion for power-sharing in the small, as well as the large, places of our lives. Together, as we confront our differences in terms of race, class, gender, and so forth, we may discover that these differences are at times a source of pain and conflict, but at other times are an unexpected source of redemption. An erotic desire for justice can open people to greater freedom and mutual respectfulness, personally as well as politically.

No matter what our social location is, the cultural crisis about sexuality is further complicated by the absence of a reliable moral tradition to guide our inquiry. Although churches often boast that they transcend culture and stand in tension with prevailing norms, the churches' struggles with sexuality reflect more than challenge the culture's dis-ease with sex and power. Conflicts within the churches serve as an accurate bellwether for gauging the depth and intensity of the cultural crisis. As ethicist James B. Nelson observes, many people within religious communities "have not been able to deal creatively and forthrightly with sexuality in virtually any form."[2] Part of this difficulty is rooted in a dualistic tradition within Christianity that fears and disparages the body and things sexual. Another factor is that many people uncritically pass on received tradition as if it represented an unassailable and permanently valuable moral truth. However, when people rely exclusively on the past to discern present realities, dehumanizing cultural patterns often go unnoticed and unchallenged.

Moral traditions are kept alive only by an ongoing process of self-criticism and reconstruction. Many religious persons, because they have been so reactive to changing cultural patterns, have not been able to revitalize their moral traditions. Moreover, whenever churches become skittish about sex and fearful of conflict, they fail, and often fail miserably, to hold onto many of their members, including those more mature adults who refuse either to stigmatize sexuality or to fall into silence in order to "keep the peace."[3] However, as the cultural influence of churches has waned, they have tenaciously grabbed hold of the family and sexuality as their last domain of authority, but because they have sought control more than fresh insight, their credibility has been eroded even more. Instead of exercising their role as cultural critics and prophetic visionaries, many church people adamantly refuse to look at change realistically. As journalist Geneva Overholser, herself the daughter of a Presbyterian minister, explains, they insist, despite all the evidence, that yesterday's mores still fit and should prevail. When churches become bastions of denial about sex or any other dimension of life, however, they risk becoming irrelevant to the cultural struggles under way.[4]

For the most part, religious communities have responded with neither creativity nor compassion to the cultural crisis in sexuality. In fact, when it comes to sex, many religious people (and institutions) are at their worst. On the one hand, they are fearful about sex; on the other hand, they become fixated on the forbidden and repressed. This interlocking dynamic of fear and fixation makes it exceedingly difficult to keep sexuality in perspective. Concerning this important, but far from consuming, dimension of human life, people vacillate between making too much ("It's everything") or too little ("It means nothing") of it. As a result, moral thinking becomes skewed.

Most cultural discourse about sexuality is fear-based, but religious discourse is often the most blatantly negative. Sexuality and erotic desire are viewed stereotypically as powerful and dangerous, requiring strong externally imposed controls. Morality is reduced to "private" matters or to a punitive code restricting sexual conduct. Religious communities, by communicating explicitly negative, often shaming messages about sexuality, attempt to control people and coerce them into compliance with moral convention. However, shaming serves only to alienate people further from religious traditions.

Although secularized sources may appear to be more open about sexuality, sex is widely commodified as a means to drive consumption and, therefore, equally alienated. Consumerism plays off people's lack of self-esteem in this culture and their fears that "being more" requires "having more." The Radical Right capitalizes on this fear, which can easily be manipulated and exteriorized as stigmatizing projections onto less powerful social groups. The Right speaks relentlessly about the body's insatiability, (feminist) women's "inordinate" desires for power, and the corrupting promiscuity of (urban, white) gay male sexuality. The Right deliberately uses erotophobia to mobilize and also distract people from criticizing the capitalist economic system. Contrary to conservative polemics, however, it is neither sexual freedom nor widespread nonconformity to traditional family patterns that is undermining community, but rather late capitalism's massive global restructuring that is creating severe dislocations and moral upheaval.

In contrast, theological liberalism communicates more positively about sexuality. Its perspective, however, is also deficient. The criticism I offer here about liberalism I offer with reluctance, for several reasons. First, theological liberalism has nurtured my own moral development. As someone who came of age in the 1960s era of the civil rights and antiwar movements, I was then, and am still now, excited, unnerved, and constantly inspired by a theological tradition that insists on the centrality of justice for any credible view of God and the world.[5] Second, liberalism has become unfashionable during a time of intense cultural reaction and is now constantly under siege. Because liberalism has strongly defended a critically informed humanism and advocated human rights, I have no desire to give legitimacy to right-wing attacks on liberalism. Whatever the deficiencies of the liberal tradition, its strengths should be preserved in any theological or ethical reconstruction. After all, liberalism is the moral tradition that has most willingly valued sexuality as an essential dimension of human dignity.

Liberalism's strength is its placement of human freedom at the core of its theological vision. Responsible moral agency to re-create the world is the primary mark of faithfulness to God. Rethinking moral meaning is encouraged as an ongoing historical task, including searching for more adequate institutional forms of love and justice. We become human by our open participation in equalizing social power relations. However, liberalism has limitations that have to date prevented the development of an adequate social ethic of sexuality. First, liberal social theory splits public from private life. Justice, it says, belongs to the public ordering of social, political, and economic power relations. Love, politically ineffectual and reduced to an affective sentiment, is restricted to private matters among intimates in a separate, autonomous interpersonal sphere. The private is sealed off from the public, the personal from the social. Moreover, sexuality is viewed as nonhistorical and subject, by and large, to natural determination. Liberalism's presuppositions, especially about female nature and a naturalized family structure, replicate a nineteenth-century white bourgeois worldview that divides social reality into man's (public) world and women's (private) space. The privatized zone of nonfreedom includes sexuality, reproduction, and the care of children, all matters judged inconsequential—and typically rendered invisible in liberal social theory—in relation to the "real" (read "manly") concerns of war, politics, career, and empire-building.

Second, liberalism leaves in place a patriarchal split between thinking and feeling, a gender-based dichotomy in which feeling, associated with women and things female, is devalued, while rationality and abstract reasoning, associated with men and things male, is prized. Liberals fear that passion and strong feeling of any kind will lead inexorably to confused thinking, biased by personal involvement and self-interest.[6] Self-assertion, self-interest, and nearly all self-love are consistently met with suspicion. Liberal social theory sees the self as basically nonsocial, self-preoccupied, and able to enter—or not enter—with others into community. It fails, however, to appreciate the limits of its culturally constructed view as the product of reified masculine consciousness. In contrast, feminist theory appreciates how all persons, male and female, are fundamentally

7

relational and social beings whose personhood is constituted in the communities upon which they depend for survival, care, and ongoing development.

Although liberalism professes to value human dignity, its tendency toward individualism places self-regard and other-regard in tension, forever in opposition. Their irreconcilable conflict, liberalism conjectures, can be resolved only by a selfless altruism or, when necessary, by self-denial. However, liberalism has not shaken free of misogyny. It continues to assign self-sacrifice selectively to women (and other socially subordinate people) and rarely invokes it as a male virtue or as an obligation for the powerful. In contrast, feminist and gay liberation perspectives encourage self-love as healthy and morally good, especially among marginalized peoples. Self-love is a corrective to internalized oppression and self-hate. Contrary to liberal fears, valuing of self and valuing of others are not mutually exclusive, antagonistic options, but rather reciprocal, fully interdependent possibilities.[7] Doing justice, in liberation perspective, is a remarkable pathway for deepening love.

Finally, liberalism by and large accepts the prevailing cultural model of power as unilateral control. Such power competes with others for scarce, limited resources. Again, this contrasts with feminist theory that envisions power as power-with and power-for others and as the humanizing capacity to sustain relationship and build community through mutual regard and care.[8]

Although liberalism insists that concern for justice should lie at the heart of any ethic, liberal Christianity has discounted oppression in the so-called private sphere and has been reluctant to integrate feminist and gay liberation insight into its own perspective. Sexuality has been depoliticized and set apart from social structures and power conflicts. Liberalism's language about love often appears idealized and disconnected from people's everyday struggles and pain. Liberalism sidesteps power and conflict within interpersonal relations and is neither clear enough nor tough enough about family violence or abuse of power among intimates. In the real world, countless women, children, and sexual minorities are at risk, especially in racial/ethnic communities and among the poor. As a gay man, although I have been nurtured by liberalism, I have also become vividly aware that this tradition makes no room for receiving me or other nonnormative peoples. Liberalism sees my struggle for self-respect as a private concern, not as a matter of justice or as a problem of disordered power.

Although relatively sex-positive in outlook, liberalism also fails to value erotic power as a significant *moral* power making intimacy possible between people and their world. Not only does liberalism fail to associate intimacy with justice, it also bypasses the deficits of love without justice. The romanticizing of marriage and idealizing of family life conceal widespread abuse and human suffering. The notion that family life is private blocks recognition of how the quality of personal life is dependent on the wider social order. Many women, however, grasp these interconnections simply by taking into account differentials in earning power and how these differently impact men and women's options, within and outside of the family. Women's economic dependence on men affects power relations within the household, and it limits access to education, employment, leisure, and community life. These disparities constrict women's freedom. At the same time, most men, especially white affluent men, feel entitled to exit any relationship when they choose, and they have the power and resources available to do so. The freedom to extricate oneself from an undesired situation, however, is denied to all but the most economically privileged women. Most women lack the independent economic resources that would allow them to break free from abusive situations and leave loveless marriages.

An ethic of sexuality must realistically assess what poor women, women of color, and other disenfranchised people are up against in this culture. The fact that many women "put up with" abuse and degradation tells us volumes, if we can hear, not about any purported female desperation to seek "love" at any cost, but rather about the devastating absence of justice and well-being in most women's lives and in the lives of their children. Those lacking social power stay in dehumanizing, often life-threatening situations not because of *personal* inadequacies but because there are few, if any, *social* alternatives that justify taking the risks of leaving an abusive but familiar situation, especially because men typically escalate their violence to keep "their" women in place.[9] Liberalism's moral guidance about sex and family life will never be useful if it leaves unquestioned the power hierarchies of husband over wife, parent over child, white over black, able-bodied over disabled, and so forth, or if it naturalizes these relationships as beneficial to all parties.

"The best theorizing about justice," feminist philosopher Susan Moller Okin writes, "is not some abstract 'view from nowhere,' but proceeds from the carefully attentive consideration of *everyone*'s point of view."[10] The strength of Okin's statement is that she insists that moral reason is concretely situated, but her claim, as it stands, is not strong enough to make a real difference in a stratified, conflicted world of power inequities. From a postliberal perspective, theorizing about sexual injustice must proceed by listening to—and giving priority to—those who are subjected to sexual oppression and who manage against all odds to resist its indignities. Listening can become justice-bearing only as the conversation is recentered and democratized. The voices of socially powerful, privileged people need to be heard, but their voices must no longer monopolize the discussion. Moral traditions can correct past distortions and become more humanizing, but only if we pay special attention to the voices and moral wisdom of women, gay/lesbian/bisexual people, survivors of sexual violence, and others without social status and power. By incorporating these voices from the margins, the liberal theological tradition can also be transformed. Perspectives from "the underside" enrich the ethical analysis, as well as stretch the vision of the moral good.

The feminist and gay liberation movements, especially as they maintain a strong commitment to race and class diversity, are shaking the foundations by their insistence on a reordering of social power toward equality, including all sexual relations. Transformative moral wisdom emerges from the collective insights of social movements as they seek, over time, to reconstruct power dynamics and renew cultural traditions. Religious communities, whether they recognize it or not, are indebted to the feminist and womanist movements and to the gay/lesbian/bisexual liberation movement for keeping alive a vision of justice within personal life. The impetus for rethinking the sexual system is coming not from established insiders but from social justice movements on the margins.

Conventional Christian moral wisdom, among liberals and conservatives alike, has encoded *elite affluent, white male* perspectives and their moral interests about sexuality. Until women's perspectives, representing a full range of class, race, and age diversity, are fully incorporated into Christian theological reflection, the dominant tradition will remain androcentric in perspective and masculinist in its values. Until the perspectives of lesbian women, gay men, and bisexual persons of differing classes, races, and ages are fully incorporated into Christian theological reflection, the tradition will suffer the limitations of being heterocentric in perspective and heterosexist in its values. Two problems will persist.

First, moral discourse, unless restructured, will alienate and disparage those outside the ranks of the elite, presumably heterosexual male authority in church and society. After completing her study of official Roman Catholic teachings on sexuality, ethicist Barbara Andolsen remarked that the entire experience was profoundly alienating. "It often meant seeing human sexual behavior," she writes, "through the eyes of men who are distrustful of women."[11] Socially powerful men consistently turn women into the devalued Other, who by definition are denied the power and the moral right to make claims on others. A similar process renders gay people invisible or turns them into objects of pity and scorn.

A second problem is that in a religious tradition so deeply conflicted about bodily existence and sexual feelings, male elites have attempted to resolve their own ambivalence by splitting off their erotic feelings and projecting them onto women, gay men, and people of color, who are then objectified as dangers to proper moral order. This trashing of women and gay people is a moral scandal that must cease, especially within religious communities. Sexualizing others may be an effective way to discredit opponents while claiming the high moral ground for oneself, but it does little to assist people in integrating sexuality into their lives or appreciating the ties between sexuality and spirituality.

In order to move beyond reactionary politics and moral conventionality about sexuality, people must enter into, not just talk about, genuine solidarity with women and gay people of all colors and with people whose bodies and spirits are routinely violated in this culture. Herein lies the rub. With respect to sexuality, most people associated with institutionalized religion have been taught to fear difference and to avoid flesh-and-blood contact with people "not like them." Lacking real-life connection with those rendered Other, they also fail to see how injustice is present in their own experience and diminishes their humanity. Out of touch with their own pain, they fail to perceive the pain of others. They become confused about the cultural crisis and frightened. How might this myopia and social paralysis be corrected?

Philosopher Iris Young makes an intriguing suggestion in speaking of feminism's central epistemological insight that a "sense of justice arises not from looking [on from a distance], but . . . from listening."[12] Constructive ethics cannot be done without listening to, and learning from, those struggling on the margins to survive on the underside of history. This move-to-the-margins places us within the bounds of a postliberal ethical method. In this alternative paradigm, theological reflection is unapologetically an advocacy project, engaged in to serve the needs of marginalized communities. Theological reflection begins not with revelation or church tradition but with the concrete sufferings of people and with a commitment to reorder personal and community life so that the suffering may end and healing may begin. There is methodological suspicion about how moral problems have been interpreted. Critical social theory is used to reinterpret the problem and analyze its ideological supports, in order to advance the interests of the disenfranchised for justice. As educator Suzanne Toten observes, first the problem must be analyzed in light of the experiential wisdom of those directly affected, and only then can we begin to reinterpret the problem in light of faith claims or begin to formulate change strategies. Such a methodological approach must remain provisional and open-ended. The moral knowledge gained in this process, as well as its truthfulness and benefits, Toten concludes, can be adequately tested only by living out its implications.[13]

Conventional moral discourse about sexuality is currently at an impasse. Because of the economic and organizational strength of the Radical Right, its highly politicized talk about restoring "traditional family" values has become exceedingly dangerous, especially for people marginalized by race, class, and nonnormative sexuality within every social group. The Right is culturally reasserting white, affluent, male hegemony as the necessary social mechanism for preserving both the family (read "male-dominated, affluent families") and the capitalist social order. A countervailing weight is needed to offset this politically reactionary movement.

Because theological liberalism has refused to be "baptized" by feminism and gay/lesbian/bisexual liberation, it has also failed to incorporate the moral wisdom of these justice movements into its own moral paradigm. Liberalism continues to sever the personal from the political, and it makes little room for passion in its quest for justice. The dichotomizing of relational life from social-structural conditions, however, and the splitting of love from justice have been liberalism's persistent failure. In order to heal these splits and bring liberalism's commitment to human freedom and well-being to greater consistency, we need a fresh, more integrated way of thinking about sexuality, about moral freedom and responsibility, and about faith communities as prophetic advocates for the disenfranchised.

The Structure of This Book

In this book I seek to construct a postliberal Christian sexual ethic by mapping an alternative framework to make sense of, and respond to, the contemporary crisis of sexuality. My intention is to offer a moral vision about sexuality that is neither fear-based nor preoccupied with control as the appropriate moral response to erotic power. Furthermore, as a chastened and now-reconstructed liberal, I contend that in our crisis-ridden world, Christianity's moral voice about these humanly important matters will only become more privatized and ineffectual unless its love ethic becomes more fully integrated with the kind of justice commitment that encompasses both the personal and the political. A revitalized, genuinely liberating moral discourse will insist that, contrary to the Right's reassertion of hierarchical control and to a much greater extent than liberalism's soft love ethic, all social relations must be reordered in the direction of equality and mutuality. This moral reordering must include our most intimate, interpersonal relationships, as well as our politics, economics, and cultural practices.

In chapter 1, I begin to reframe the moral conversation by naming sexuality as a justice issue. I am proposing a shift in Christian ethical thinking from a love-centered liberal ethic, which privatizes sexuality as a concern individuals must manage on their own, to a justice-centered liberating ethic that connects people's personal pains (and joys) with larger socio-cultural dynamics that either frustrate or enhance communal well-being. Our sexualities, that is, our embodied capacities for love and intimacy, are strengthened or diminished in community with others, and it is in and through the reshaping of our communities that our personal well-being is most powerfully affected.

In chapter 2, I provide a structural analysis of how sexuality in a racist, patriarchal culture has become intertwined with ableism, racism, sexism, and heterosexism. When eroticism is annexed by social injustice, our capacity to love expansively is impeded. Chapter 2 critiques the prevailing sexual ideology and its ethic of body control and ownership.

Chapter 3 identifies resources for a liberating ethic of sexuality. Because of Christianity's sex-negativity and moralistic, controlling bent with respect to sexual expression, traditional Christian teachings must be critiqued. I wager that Christian moral tradition may be enlarged and transformed by incorporating new voices from the margins and joining with them in their justice struggles for dignity and communal well-being. The question I ask is, What would a profeminist, gay-positive, and antiracist rereading of Christian tradition offer for the renewal of Christian sexual ethics?

Chapter 4 critiques how traditionalists, libertarians, and liberals frame sexual ethics. I then construct an alternative Christian ethic of sexuality that is sex-positive and antiabuse. This reframed ethic affirms our common humanity across differences of race, gender, class, and sexual orientation. It also challenges traditional, fear-based moralities that focus on control of persons and their bodies. In contrast, an alternative liberating ethic empowers people for responsible freedom.

Chapter 5 provides a test case for judging the adequacy of this proposed justice-love ethic of sexuality. I address men's violence against women, children, and other men. As a justice-seeking man within a male supremacist culture, I long for a liberating way to be both self-respecting as a man and also justly connected with others. I argue that to make gains in this direction, men must take responsibility to work with other men in order to stop intimate violence and disentangle men's sexuality from violence and injustice.

In the conclusion I explore how patriarchal Christianity disconnects spirituality from sexuality, as well as the ethical implications of reclaiming an erotic, sensuous spirituality of body justice. The moral wisdom of gay, lesbian, and bisexual persons is a primary resource for revitalizing religious traditions and refocusing them on things that matter. In our time, spiritual renewal within our faith communities, as well as our own moral integrity, are inextricably dependent upon committing ourselves to courageous advocacy, sustained over the long haul, for sexual and other forms of justice. We nurture our spirits by embracing the body as sacred, inviolate territory.

When all this is said, however, the moral project before us is not to arrive at a new understanding of sexuality or erotic justice, but rather to embody this justice concretely in our lives and in our loving. Biblical scholar Walter Brueggemann writes, "One is enjoined to *do justice* as God does justice. And when God does justice, it is not modest or polite or understated. It is an act of powerful intervention. It is like Moses in the court of Pharaoh insisting on freedom."[14] God is a lover of justice, and our calling is to be passionate justice lovers in all and through all.

My goal in this book is to sketch the outlines of an erotic ethic of justice-love and to begin to color in its contours.[15] Such an ethic, I believe, will enlarge and perhaps revitalize liberal discourse as it incorporates and benefits from the moral wisdom of women, gay people, and other "strangers" on the margins. Liberating moral discourse about sexuality must rejoin what has been tragically rendered asunder: on the one hand, our longing for pleasure, joy, and at-homeness in our bodies and, on the other hand, our desire for justice and well-being throughout our social world. A liberating social ethic of sexuality places great value on the humanly powerful desire for intimacy and community. It appreciates the fact that when we seek erotic justice, we often find amazing pleasure and real refreshment, as well as renewed energy to engage our world and make a difference. Our pursuit of erotic justice allows us, much to our delight, to make a remarkable, life-enhancing, and at times life-saving discovery: our deepest yearnings for love and well-being can be satisfied only as we enlarge our commitments to doing justice—*passionately*—with one another or, put in more traditional language, only as we devote ourselves, in a wholehearted, full-bodied way, to loving God, each other, and this precious, fragile planet with all our soul and strength.

Rethinking Sexuality

An Issue of Justice

Sexual justice [is] the most trivialized, feared,
and postponed dimension of social justice in
western society and, possibly, in the world.[1]
                                      —Carter Heyward

An ethic of sexuality should help people make sense of their social world, open up fresh insight, and promote personal and social well-being. The appropriate starting point for developing such an ethic is to analyze the sociohistorical context in which the contemporary crisis of sexuality has emerged.

Moral panics about sexuality routinely surface today. Widespread fear of moral decline, the demise of the family, and pending social collapse give rise to ongoing "sex debates" in the culture. Highly conflicted views circulate and clash about sexuality, its meaning and its proper place in human life. Three different viewpoints—traditionalist, libertarian, and liberal—have played off each other and shaped moral discourse about human sexuality, but none of them recognizes sexuality as a justice issue. To correct that deficiency, it is important to listen to and learn from voices from the underside of history and Christian tradition, including feminists, survivors of sexual violence, and gay/lesbian/bisexual persons, who all are pressing for a reconstruction of Christian sexual ethics. An alternative, liberating moral discourse about sexuality, deeply informed by their voices, not only clarifies some basic dimensions of sexual injustice. It also lifts up a normative vision of sexual justice as embodied right-relatedness. Overcoming sexual alienation is an indispensable component of any liberating moral project because every oppression involves violence toward the devalued body.

Sexuality:
A Crisis within a Crisis

Making sense of the current crisis of sexuality requires exploring the cultural context in which this turmoil is brewing. At the close of the twentieth century, we are witnessing an extended, historically complex period of restructuring in which social relations are being reorganized politically, economically, and culturally. Four hundred years ago, turbulent disruptions marked the emergence of a modern world in the West and the development of market economies, nation-states, and a religious reformation. Today, an equally disruptive process of structural reorganizing is going on, fueled by the accelerating integration of national economies into a global economy. A new world order is moving into place. Willingly or not, we are entering a postmodern world marked by widespread human suffering, as well as by massive resistance to this entire process.

In response to this crisis, liberation movements among the poor and marginalized throughout the globe are sparking radical new social visions of communal survival and renewal. Popular movements are gathering momentum, binding together spirituality and justice-making and calling for genuinely inclusive, egalitarian communities. A grassroots, broadbased movement for sexual justice is one component of this global movement for renewal. Sexual justice-making seeks procreative rights for women and protection from forced sterilization; the end of international sex tourism; passage and enforcement of gay/lesbian civil rights; increased legal and social resources for sexually abused children and adults, including elders and incapacitated adults; expanded sexuality education programs; high quality, affordable childcare and eldercare; increased social services for rape victims and legal enforcement of antirape laws; continued theological and liturgical renewal in feminist and womanist modes; and so forth.

This multidimensional crisis of economic, political, and cultural restructuring is the proper context in which to analyze the crisis of sexuality. Within this broader cultural restructuring, there is a crisis of sexual relations. This crisis in sexuality is not a discrete or autonomous set of problems, but is rather a process embedded in and affected by changes happening at many other levels. The crisis of sexuality is revealed, in part, by persistently distorted, highly negative attitudes about sex, the human body, women, and other marginalized people. Other indicators include a booming pornography industry, pervasive patterns of sexual assault and abuse, the ordinariness of antigay/antilesbian violence, and the social anxiety which accompanies an epidemic spread of sexually transmitted disease, including HIV infection.

The heart of this crisis of sexuality lies in the massive social conflict over reordering men and women's power and gender roles and in the resistance to ending male violence and control of women and children. The feminist liberation movement, calling for gender justice in the family and throughout the social order, including faith communities, insists that issues of power and control be addressed within interpersonal and all other social relations, especially those structured by race and class. An entire cultural ideology about gender, sexuality, and family is being questioned. A 1991 Presbyterian study names this crisis "a massive cultural earthquake, a loosening of the hold of an unjust, patriarchal structure built on dehumanizing assumptions, roles, and relationships. This unjust structure," the report concludes, "stifles human well-being and stands in contradiction to the gospel mandate to love God and neighbor as self."[2]

Previously taken-for-granted beliefs about male and female roles, about the relation of sex and procreation to marriage, and about duty and pleasure are being contested. Fundamental rethinking is going on about moral expectations and how to distinguish acceptable from unacceptable behavior. Conflict also rages, not surprisingly, about sources and authority for a sexual ethic. Should there be a realignment of values, and if so, who is entitled to reconfigure the moral boundary markers? What changes should be supported, even embraced, and which ones resisted? What theologian Margaret Farley says about Roman Catholicism is true for other religious traditions, as well as for the culture at large: "Nearly every traditional moral rule governing sexual behavior in Western culture is today being challenged." The morality of same-sex relations is the most "intensely probed" and "politically volatile" issue[3] and has become a bellwether for the cultural crisis.

Moral Panics

Cultural crisis, social disruption, and escalating uncertainty bring fear. Because of the protracted nature of our contemporary crisis, this fear will not likely abate any time soon. Economic dislocation produces community disintegration and a rise in social violence. Hate crimes are on the increase against marginalized communities, including sexual minorities. Most people face a growing disparity between their personal power to shape the future and the power of institutions. Increasing numbers of people lack adequate economic power to support their families. Their fear, often expressed as social panic, is warranted, but why does this fear become attached to sexuality? Why do economic and other forms of insecurity translate into sexual rigidity?

Crosscultural studies indicate that the human body often symbolizes and, therefore, stands in for the corporate body politic. "Just as it is true that everything symbolizes the body," explains anthropologist Mary Douglas, "so it is equally true (and all the more so for that reason) that the body symbolizes everything else." Social tensions are writ small on the human body. "For example," Douglas continues, "there are beliefs that each sex is a danger to the other through contact with sexual fluids. . . . Such patterns of sexual danger can be seen to express symmetry or hierarchy. It is implausible to interpret them as expressing something about the actual relation of the sexes. I suggest that many ideas about sexual dangers are better interpreted as symbols of the relation between parts of society, as mirroring designs of hierarchy or symmetry which apply in the larger social system."[4]

When rapid social change occurs, social dis-ease can readily surface as fear about sexuality, moral chaos, and the disintegration of family life. Sociologists observe that the sexual revolution in the 1960s accelerated a change process that for more than a century has been unsettling established boundaries around personal life and sexual activity. People rally in defense of or in critique of family life because, as sociologist Jeffrey Weeks suggests, they attach critical importance to "boundary maintenance in staving off challenges to social status and sexual identity."[5] Sexuality and family life are areas in which many people expect to have control and believe they can make a difference.

Although fears about the disappearance of marriage and family are largely unfounded, anxiety persists in a time of rapid social change. Deep currents of social sentiment often surface as moral panics. Such panics are not new. During the 1880s, with the massive social disruptions caused by urban industrialization, moral crusades were launched to stop vice. Purity campaigns, largely aimed at bolstering middle-class influence with immigrants and the working poor, sought to outlaw prostitution and end the practice of masturbation. During the 1950s, at the height of the Cold War, social fears about communism focused on the "homosexual menace" and juvenile delinquency. In our own tumultuous time, welfare recipients, urban (black) youth, feminists, and gay/lesbian/bisexual people are the targets of right-wing attack.[6]

Moral panics, whether focused explicitly on family or on sex and eroticism, gain momentum by associating sexuality with disorder, filth, disease, and danger. Anxiety about social change can be easily manipulated, as we see clearly in current church-based debates over homosexuality and abortion. This is hardly surprising given the fact that churches are also facing enormous structural change, especially older mainline Protestant churches whose cultural hegemony has long been on the wane. Declines in membership and in public authority have generated panic within religious communities that, in reaction, resort to sexual repression in order to deal with structural upheaval.

Typically, social fear crystallizes around a particular group or condition that becomes the Other, a perceived threat to established values. The social panic over AIDS as a "gay plague" illustrates this pattern. Karen

Bloomquist, a Lutheran theologian, observes that in debates concerning sexuality, "the overwhelming tendency is to focus or even become fixated on the sexuality of those the dominant group considers to be 'other' than themselves." Many men become obsessive about women's power. Married persons scrutinize the sex lives of single persons (or of other married people who do marriage differently). Heterosexual persons focus on gay men and lesbians. Gay men and lesbians may fret over bisexual and transgender people. A defensive, largely unconscious strategy, Bloomquist suggests, keeps "the problem 'out there' so that [people] do not have to face [their] own fears connected with the most intimate aspects of [their] lives."[7]

Moral panics point to strongly contested areas of human life around which social anxieties can be quickly displaced onto the "frail reed" of human sexuality. Sociologist James Davison Hunter describes the battles raging over sexuality as cultural contests about what constitutes normative family and cultural authority (what are the rules for sexual intimacy, and who gets to define and enforce them?). As Hunter explains, "cultural conflict is about power—a struggle to achieve or maintain the power to define reality."[8] In the midst of cultural crisis, sex and sexuality are, therefore, far from being frivolous, inconsequential matters that detract attention from the so-called weightier issues of poverty, environmental destruction, racism, and war. At a time when human suffering nearly exceeds our moral imagination's ability to grasp, we must regain moral perspective about our lives-in-relation, including our intimate connections, and must offset the tendency many people express when, out of panic and often pain, they either blame themselves or look outward for enemies and scapegoats. Attending to sexuality is morally imperative because, as anthropologist Gayle S. Rubin points out, in this environment "people are likely to become dangerously crazy about sexuality." "Consequently," she cautions, "sexuality should be treated with special respect in times of great social stress."[9] Matters of value, meaning, and purpose are at stake. Survival is also at stake for marginalized peoples.[10]

Voices in the Dominant Moral Discourse about Sex: Traditionalist, Libertarian, Liberal

Traditionalists, libertarians, and liberals offer competing messages about good and bad sex, but each voice reflects fear about sexuality and seeks control directly (traditionalists), in reaction to (libertarians), or because of ambivalence about sex (liberals). All three engage in what James Davison Hunter calls "culture wars," an intense battle rooted in competing moral visions about personal and social life. Each promotes a conception of the good society, the good and morally decent person, and the properly constituted family.

Sexual traditionalists interpret the crisis of sexuality in terms of the abandonment of traditional values. They offer dire warnings about the loss of established authority and urge a return to an ethic of "moral normalcy." Present troubles, they argue, stem from widespread disregard of long-standing, conventional controls needed to channel human sexuality in safe, familiar directions. Sexually active teenagers, single mothers, and gay men and lesbian women are particularly troubling because these groups flaunt nonconformity and violate the norms traditionalists see as God-given for natural, normal sex, that is, sex that is heterosexual and procreative in intent. Nonconformity to traditional male authority undermines family life and, by extension, the social order. Morality requires confining sexual behavior exclusively to male-controlled heterosexual marriage. Good order requires "celibacy in singleness, sex only in marriage."

Voices of conformity long for a romanticized past of cultural homogeneity, mythically populated by white, affluent, heterosexual Protestants in suburban families. Politically active traditionalists seek to restore sexuality to an exclusively marital, reproductive context. By opposing legalized abortion, the distribution of contraceptives, and sex education in public schools, they hope to reassert their cultural hegemony. Fearful of sexual anarchy, their moral watchword is control. Their major concern is holding deviance in check. For traditionalists, male control and female submission remain normative expectations.

Sexual libertarians emerged during the 1920s and 1960s, both eras of sharp challenge to conventional morality in which a cultural consensus began to emerge that sexual pleasure is basic to human fulfillment.[11] Libertarians advocate a minimalist ethic. They mandate consent between sexual partners, but ask few questions about context, power dynamics, or social consequences. Sexual libertarians argue for unrestricted sexual freedom and the easing of institutional regulations about sex, including laws regulating pornography, prostitution, and intergenerational sex. By emphasizing sex freed from fear, guilt, and shame, they contribute significantly to the ethical debate on sex, but by overreacting to moralistic controls, they promote a sexuality magically freed from social consequences and, therefore, exempt from moral evaluation.

A third voice, sexual liberalism, is sounded by progressive Christians, among others. Liberals express discontent with traditional morality, but also show reservations about sex, women's power and full emancipation, and homosexuality as a legitimate "lifestyle." Like libertarians, liberals praise the goodness of sexuality but hedge their bets about whether eroticism is morally good. Like traditionalists, liberals fear that sexuality, especially in its nonnormative forms, will tempt people to violate moral boundaries and succumb to irresponsible, even dangerous, pleasures. Liberals operate with a domino theory of sexual peril. A precariously maintained line of moral propriety differentiates good sex from bad sex and what is safe from what is ultimately dangerous. This line is drawn to prevent people from crossing over a moral threshold and risking ruin. According to the liberal worldview, restraint must hold sexual desire in check because, as feminist philosopher Mariana Valverde explains, "there is in every human being an inborn sinfulness, an inherent tendency to slide down the [slippery] slope unless held in check by such external constraints as priestly authority, legal punishment, fear of hell, and last but not least, fear of social stigma." This negative anthropology views sexual feelings as potent carriers of illicit desire, and for this reason, many religious people do not differentiate between sin and sexuality. "It is this idea," Valverde suggests, that "lends a quality of desperation to much of Christian moral theory."[12]

This liberal moral framework about sexual pleasure and danger has influenced debates about masturbation, oral and anal sex, prostitution, consensual sadomasochistic sex, and pornography. Many people fear that sexual freedom, unless carefully contained, will inexorably lead to excess and moral turpitude. In a repressive, sex-preoccupied culture, many internalize in their psyches and in their bodies their anxiety about social disorder as a palpable fear of sex. Even relatively innocent sexual pleasures, it is feared, might lead to excess and, ultimately, to depravity, social aggression, and even sadomasochistic violence. Some gay men, for example, struggle with their own internalized homophobia and avoid intimacy with other men because of a culturally inculcated fear that homosexual desire will "naturally" degenerate and place them in jeopardy of engaging in acts they abhor and stand little risk of doing, including pedophilia. Similarly, some people fear that any social acceptance of sexually explicit erotica will open the door to, and then fail to limit, the worst kinds of violent, morally degrading pornographic materials. Although the particular example of potentially offending desire may differ from person to person, the unexamined assumption here is that people stand precariously balanced at the edge of a moral precipice. Because too much sex, too many desires, and too much bodiliness threaten to send people over the edge into social chaos, they learn to fear their desires and mistrust their capacities as morally self-directing agents. In the liberal imagination, sex may be good (at least in some forms), but it is also at least potentially dangerous and fraught with anxiety.

Conventional sexual ethics, even in liberal form, is fueled by such sex-negativity. Because liberals are ambivalent about the moral goodness of eroticism, they too insist on keeping a framework of control. Sex is good or, at least, legitimate sex is good if it is heterosexual, institutionalized and regulated within marriage, monogamous, reproductive, and noncommercial. In contrast to traditionalists, liberals give latitude to sexually active single people if they do not explicitly reject marriage or question normative heterosexuality. Liberalism fails, however, to question its basic framework of sexual fear and control. Only those activities on the "good side" of the moral line, that is, within heterosexual monogamous marriage, are granted moral complexity or given the benefit of involving authentic affection and free choice. "In contrast," sociologist Gayle Rubin notes, "all sexual acts on the bad side of the line are considered utterly repulsive and devoid of all emotional nuance." In fact, "the further from the line a sex act is, the more it is depicted as a uniformly bad experience."[13]

By reinforcing a sex-negative framework, liberalism reinforces people's fear not only of sex, but also of stepping out of bounds. They become fixated on what is prohibited to them rather than on what causes authentic pleasure for them or their partners. People learn to mistrust themselves, but also to be suspicious of others, especially sexual misfits who fail to measure up to conventional standards. Gay, lesbian, and bisexual people who are "out and proud," as well as pregnant teenagers and sexually active welfare mothers, represent the preeminent sexual outlaws in this culture. They have broken with the conventional controls on sexuality and "flaunt" moral decency. One consequence of this control system is that prevailing sexual moral discourse, in both its conservative and liberal guises, remains overwhelmingly judgmental, fear-ridden, and punitive. Another consequence is that people become both self-hating and pleasure deprived. When deprived of pleasure and especially pleasurable touch, people are not only more prone to violence, but also more compliant with external authorities. What a tragic state of affairs! A postliberal ethic appreciates how the absence of genuine pleasure in people's lives is a significant, though often neglected, dimension of human oppression.

What traditionalists, libertarians, and liberals lack, in their own way, is an animating quest for sexual justice. Coming of age about sexuality requires the ability to affirm a diversity of responsible sexualities, including those of gay men, lesbians, and bisexuals, as well as to appreciate the strengths of nontraditional families. Sexual traditionalists, however, make little room for diversity. Their inclination is to punish, not welcome, pluralism and difference. Libertarians, on the other hand, fail to emphasize how freedom, sexual or otherwise, is securely constructed only on the foundation of justice as right-relatedness and mutual respect among persons and groups. Freedom is not license, but rather is grounded in responsibility to be with and for one another in community. Responsible freedom promotes the well-being of self *and* others within relations of mutual accountability, safety, and care. Liberalism's strength is its commitment to protect individual rights and avoid policing personal conduct (until that conduct infringes on the rights of others or jeopardizes public safety). Liberalism's weakness, however, is its discounting of structural injustices with regard to sexuality and the negative impact of these injustices on personal life. It minimizes sexual oppression, as well as how power dynamics within intimate relations reinforce larger social patterns of injustice.

Each of these voices—traditionalist, libertarian, and liberal—has influenced church debates and teachings about sexuality. The missing voices are the voices from the margins, calling for justice and for a reintegration of relational and structural dynamics.

Getting to New Moral Insight

No sexual ethic will be helpful or credible until those most affected by sexual injustice directly shape the moral discourse. This epistemological claim has important implications. Fresh moral insight emerges out of social struggle. Social justice movements, including the antiracist feminist, womanist, mujerista, and gay liberation movements, are concrete, flesh-and-blood locales for new moral vision. Fresh moral insight is generated by communal effort to reorder alienating conditions, including morally inadequate religious traditions, sustained over time. Resisting injustice gives an epistemological advantage to those on the underside. "Just as someone coming in from outside is better able to tell those inside how stuffy a room has become," theologian William Sloane Coffin observes, "so women and minorities are better able to gauge the injustices of our society."[14] The battered women's movement illustrates this claim well. Within two decades this grassroots social-change movement, largely the work of formerly battered women, has organized a global network of shelters and community resources to meet the needs of women for safety, support, and public advocacy. By breaking socially sanctioned silence about abuse, by respecting women's moral courage and tenacity, and by recognizing women's stories as the primary resource for making sense of men's violence against women and children, women have developed sophisticated social theory and policy analysis out of their political work of empowering themselves.[15] In doing so, they have exhibited what feminist scholar Elizabeth Janeway calls the two distinctive "powers of the weak"—the power of disbelief and the power of coming together.[16] Disbelief encourages the questioning of official interpretations that mask social oppression and grant legitimacy to the status quo. Coming together, the joining of diverse people out of mutual respect and shared determination to remake community, grants the disenfranchised both voice and power.

Those who exercise these "powers of the weak" are changing Christian moral discourse about sexuality. Sometimes noisily, sometimes quietly, they are challenging the normativity of procreative heterosexuality, the widespread patterns of sexual violence and abuse of power, and the cultural preoccupation with control rather than enhancement of intimacy relations. Lesbian and nonlesbian women, gay men, and survivors of sexual and domestic violence of all colors are coming together and dramatically reframing moral discourse about sexuality and personal/family life.

Dimensions of Sexual Injustice

How should a justice-centered ethic of sexuality be framed? We must begin by (1) listening to and learning from those who are marginalized by present patterns of social power and privilege and (2) reenvisioning sexuality to reflect the complexity and diversity of the full human community. In an open-ended process of moral reimagination, we must address three dimensions of sexual injustice.

First, sex-negativity is pervasive in Western culture. Sexuality is intrinsic to our humanness and dignity as persons. Ethicist James B. Nelson writes, "Sexuality always involves more than what we do with our genitals." It is "who we are as body-selves who experience the emotional, cognitive, physical, and spiritual need for intimate communion, both creaturely and divine."[17] This positive notion contrasts with prevailing cultural assumptions that sex is a destructive force, that the body is inferior to the mind and spirit, and that sexual desire threatens to violate every boundary.

Sex-negative messages are communicated widely in this culture. The body is considered inferior, and genitalia or "private parts" are regarded as particularly dirty, unruly, and wrong to touch. Right order is presumed to require the superior spirit/mind to exercise watchful control over the inferior, wayward body. What we repress, however, becomes what we obsess about. The body/spirit dualism accustoms people to thinking of the body as an instrument to be used and exploited but seldom recognized as intrinsic to one's selfhood. Pleasures from the "lower realm," Nelson explains, are not easily integrated into one's image of a moral self.[18]

A second dualism, that of gender, posits radical difference between males and females, elevates men over women, and insists that proper gender order requires male control. This gender dualism, deeply intertwined with the spiritualistic or body/spirit dualism in white Western culture, associates maleness with superior rational capacity and spiritual authority and femaleness with body, emotion, and sensuality.

Western Christian tradition is replete with testimonies about the extensive, sometimes frantic efforts by men to preserve the loftiness of their spiritual experience by distancing themselves from sexuality and by avoiding sexual pollution from women. One legacy of male clerical celibacy is the cultural belief that repudiation of body desire and disconnection from women guarantee safety and protection for men's elite status. Even though the Protestant Reformers, beginning in the sixteenth century, reclaimed the practice of clerical marriage, they did not resolve or transcend dualistic assumptions about the body and gender relations. Instead, the sexual dualisms were modified in the guise of male-female complementarity within a hierarchical male gender order. Women were assigned the subordinate role of carrying (male) cultural ambivalence about the body, sensuality, and erotic desire. Accordingly, females in this culture are categorized either as (relatively) safe (because powerless) or as dangerous (needing to be controlled, that is, disempowered). The options for women, in men's imaginations and often in social fact, have been the spiritually-minded virgin/mother/wife or the carnal whore/sensuous loose woman. Christian women were, of course, expected to be dutiful wives and good mothers, alert and responsive to male needs, humbly obedient to male authority, receptive to their subordination to male leadership, and ready to embrace their servitude in gratitude as something "for their own good" and pleasing to God.

The second dimension of sexual injustice is heterocentrism and compulsory heterosexuality. Heterocentrism, the conviction that heterosexuality alone is normal and ideal, is at the core of gay/lesbian/bisexual oppression. Thus heterosexuality becomes the definitive measure by which all other sexualities are judged.[19] Compulsory heterosexuality or heterosexism, the institutionalization of heterosexuality, enforces heterosexual norms on all persons and stigmatizes any nonconformity.

Compulsory heterosexuality reinforces both sex-negativity and the hatred of women. If erotic power is dangerous and must be contained, and if women are not self-disciplined in sex and must be controlled, where is it possible to establish safety, and how? A patriarchal church and culture have identified male-dominant heterosexual marriage as this safe place. Marriage has been designated as the proper site for containing and regulating sexual desire by controlling women's lives and specifically women's bodies. Legal codes have historically regulated marriage as an economic institution as well as a sexual arrangement, protecting men's property rights over women, children, and slaves. Such laws have provided means to establish and dissolve marriages, all with the purpose of maintaining the husband/father's control as head of family with authority over his dependents. Rules and regulations about sexuality have been framed to uphold male ownership rights within the institution of marriage. Scrutiny has continued about whether sex, especially women's sexual activity, is legitimate, that is, marital and reproductive. In fact, Christian sexual ethics have traditionally been *an ethics of marriage, not an ethics of sexuality*. The focus has been on encouraging marriage and prohibiting, or at least restricting, all nonmarital and usually all nonprocreative sexual activity.

Even within compulsory heterosexuality, erotic passion is morally suspect, but it cannot be entirely avoided given the need to regenerate the species. If sex cannot be dispensed with entirely, however, it can be redeemed if pursued not for its own sake (for pleasure alone) but for a legitimate moral purpose outside itself, namely, procreation—or, alternately, in order to strengthen the marriage bond. By this logic, there must always be a pretext for erotic pleasure. A specific reason must be found for exempting sexual activity from moral approbation. Furthermore, sexual pleasures are burdened with an excess of significance. These pleasures require justification in a way that other pleasures do not require, pleasures such as playing ensemble jazz, team bowling, duet piano playing, and gardening.[20]

Heterocentrism is in force whenever heterosexuality is naturalized as the proper destination of normal sexual development and when achievement of adult status coincides with establishing a marriage to a properly gendered "opposite" partner. Since sex is dangerous and people transgress the restrictions established for avoiding these dangers, clear strictures and steady compliance are necessary in order to minimize personal ruin and social collapse. Sex therefore takes on excessive significance and moral import. Few deviations are of little consequence. Any departure from normative heterosexuality elicits disapproval, and only marital sex is presumed to reflect the full complexity and meaning of human love and intimacy.

The third dimension of sexual injustice is the enforcement, through violence and social sanctions, of compulsory heterosexuality and of women's subordination and the eroticizing of nonmutual relations. Prevailing sexual regulations place married, reproductive heterosexuals at the top of an erotic pyramid looking down upon those who deviate from this norm. Those considered to be Other are subject to increasing degrees of disfavor, depending on how far below the summit of moral propriety they stand. Ideally from this perspective, good sex is heterosexual, marital, monogamous, and reproductive. Moral failure, however, can intrude into one or more of these categories. For example, sexually active, unmarried heterosexual couples can expect only provisional approval, but if they plan to marry or, in the case of divorce, to remarry, they gain higher moral standing. Sexually active singles who are heterosexual but not moving toward marriage have less standing and lose even more ground if they have multiple sexual partners. Within these gradations, persons across all categories receive pressure, even with threats of violence, to conform to conventional gender roles and to enter into the institution of male-dominant heterosexual marriage. Heterosexual marriage is therefore far from being a free and voluntary personal choice; it is a political requirement for normative status in this culture.

Such a sexual system distributes rewards and punishments in the interest of perpetuating a pyramidal heterosexist order and reinforcing its naturalized vision of the good. Married, heterosexual partners receive various social privileges, including social status, tax deductions, and a range of partnership rights. Gay men and lesbians are objectified as morally degenerate (defined exclusively by our sexuality) and penalized with everything from social ostracism to police harassment. Independent women are also stigmatized, especially lesbian mothers who are sexually active and those married women/mothers who are sexually active with partners other than their husbands. Sexual/erotic outlaws are threatened with penalties including the loss of employment, of family and children, of safety, mental health, and the right to contribute to the common good. Many nonconformists also fear the loss of credibility—that they will no longer be respected and have their opinions taken seriously. As Suzanne Pharr, a community activist and feminist theorist, observes, "Any one of these essential components of a full life," from jobs to safety, from family to credibility, "is large enough to make one deeply fear its loss."[21] Fear causes people to accept, or at least to fail to resist, the social controls imposed on them.

A shame-based moral system does not encourage freedom and self-confidence, nor does it promote honest and open communication with others. Fear of rejection and social ostracism also does not smooth the way for pleasure or being at ease in one's body. Antigay and antilesbian violence enforce the sexual status quo by punishing gay men and lesbians and by warning nongays to stay in line. Such violence, routine in this culture, shows the extent to which sexual alienation has become normalized. Even more telling, however, is how people's moral imaginations have become desensitized. As Gayle Rubin observes, "I would call this system of erotic stigma the last socially respectful form of prejudice" if it were not for the fact that the "old forms [of racism, sexism, etc.] show such obstinate vitality."[22]

An Alternative Vision of Possibility

The feminist and gay/lesbian/bisexual liberation movements are calling for a reordering of human sexuality toward erotic justice. But what might that look like? Two words of caution are in order. First, any moral vision will be partial, limited, and necessarily open to ongoing revision. Not everyone is yet included at the table. Furthermore, reflections on justice, as ethicist Karen Lebacqz suggests, must begin by facing the reality of injustice. "I have long been convinced," she writes, "that injustice is our lived reality, and that it is therefore the primary category." The reality of injustice is "the only honest place to begin."[23] Second, justice-making requires that people name whether their moral interests are in preserving or transforming the prevailing sexual system. Personal openness to change is not enough. Only an explicitly oppositional stance can stimulate the moral imagination and sustain people to correct whatever places them at risk. This kind of justice-making is not a "doing for others," but rather involves our willingness to be changed personally as we seek to change social conditions.

From my vantage point as a gay man claiming his self-respect in community with others, erotic justice has three fundamental dimensions:

First, advocating erotic justice in the face of sex-negativity requires honoring the goodness of sexuality as human embodiment. Sexuality is our remarkable capacity to give and receive pleasure, comfort, and mutual care through our bodies and through sensuous touch. Erotic desire, the longing to touch and be touched, is intrinsic to our well-being. Erotic desire enriches our connections to ourselves, to others, and to God, the power of "in-betweenness." Eros, when tenderly respected and responsibly directed, is a powerful, often unsettling spiritual resource.

Second, advocating erotic justice in the face of heterocentrism and compulsory heterosexuality involves genuine gratitude for difference and diversity. Diversity of age, gender, sexual orientation, color, body shape and size, family (and marital) patterns, and customs enriches, rather than diminishes, our common life. Tolerating or reluctantly accepting difference is not enough. Justice requires promoting and delighting in such diversity.

Third, advocating erotic justice in the face of sexual violence and coercion requires empowering the moral agency of the sexually abused and violated and also requires the eroticizing of equality between persons and among groups. Justice-making must focus on a fair distribution of power and social resources, but also on enhancing the safety, respect, and freedom of persons, especially those most vulnerable. Affirmations about the goodness of sex must be held in tension with an equally vivid awareness of the pain, confusion, exploitation, and grief that so many people experience. Sexual injustice is a bitter experience for many women, marginalized men, and children. Persons of color and those without some measure of economic security are often triply at risk. Our integrity as people of faith depends on showing genuine solidarity and concrete accountability to those who suffer—and to those who actively resist—sexual oppression.

If we are moved by a compelling vision of erotic justice, and if we take sexual injustice seriously as a moral problem, then we must be prepared to face and critically analyze the many configurations of injustice mediated through race, gender, and other differences. I turn in chapter 2 to this multidimensional analysis of sexuality and the social order.

2

Facing the Moral Problem
The Eroticizing of Power and Control

> Our sexuality embodies the
> injustice of our society.[1]
> —Sheila Briggs

Liberating moral discourse about sexuality must ask how racism, sexism, and other forms of oppression misshape human loving and diminish the desire for community. Sexuality is a relational-structural issue, not private but rather personal and political. We live in a web of social relationships and develop our sexualities only within institutions and systems. A social ethic of sexuality must examine how these social structures and belief systems affect our sexualities for good and ill.

A persistent failure of religious communities is that they speak about sex in an essentialist mode, ignoring the social context that gives meaning to all social interaction. Understanding sexuality as a justice issue requires analyzing the power inequalities within which persons are socialized as sexual beings. Sexuality is shaped ideologically. It is culturally encoded to reflect and reinforce existing power relations, and people either passively accept, actively promote, or intentionally resist power hierarchies along the lines of race, gender, class and other social stratification.

Human desire is in trouble in this culture. The dominant sexual code, rather than promoting the humanly good desire for intimacy and community, deforms and corrupts our desire for love. This cultural code expresses contempt for the body; devalues race, gender, and sexual difference; and is fixated on ownership and control. Because our moral power to give and receive love is misshapen at such a fundamental level, literally "next to our skins," few people learn how to be genuinely at home in their bodies or to connect respectfully with others. Instead they are taught to eroticize power inequalities as something that feels good and right.

Although religious communities by and large have failed to grasp the depth and scope of this moral problematic, feminist social analysis has begun to inform the thinking of some regarding these matters. As feminist philosopher Mariana Valverde observed more than a decade ago, however, "the debate on sexuality has not been one of the success stories of the women's movement. . . . The mere mention of the word 'sex' is more likely to cause anxiety and create suspicion than to generate solidarity and hope for the future."[2] Even the best work to date has not cast the problem broadly enough or managed to incorporate analysis of race and class as well as gender. Such a comprehensive analysis remains the collaborative work of a pluralistic, culturally diverse justice community and cannot be mapped out here. It is important to emphasize, nonetheless, that gender power inequity is only one among several other serious inequities people experience. A liberating social ethic should not privilege a gender analysis of sexuality or focus on gender to the exclusion of other factors including race and class that might determine more decisively some life situations and place those persons at risk in this culture. Race and class oppression are potent factors in creating sexual injustice, and vice versa.

In the following analysis, I have chosen to look first at how disability and race shape the dominant sexual code before I consider the impact of male gender supremacy and compulsory heterosexuality. I also want to call attention to the fact that in a culture both fearful of and fixated with sexuality, people not only psychically internalize negative attitudes about their bodies and about sex, but also literally somatize, that is, take into and upon their bodies, the effects of social oppression. Race, gender, class, and other forms of oppression condition how people feel inside their own skin, how they do (or do not) move their bodies, and how they interact with others similar to and different from themselves. However, examining the physically embodied character of social injustice both personally and corporately is often neglected in addressing the contemporary cultural crisis. Therefore, a liberating social ethic of sexuality must criticize not only unloving acts, but also unjust structures of alienating power and their ideological supports if we are to reclaim as the animating passion for our lives an erotic ethic of justice-love.

Sexuality as a Structural Problem

Moral conflict about sexuality mirrors a more generalized social conflict about power and the proper ordering of social relations. Sexuality and its patterned meanings take shape within, and become part of, this sociocultural conflict. Sociologist Jeffrey Weeks has likened sexuality to a transmission belt, constantly in motion and transmitting energy. Sexuality is able to convey a wide range of needs and desires, including "love and anger, tenderness and aggression, intimacy and adventure, romance and predatoriness, pleasure and pain, empathy and power." The expressiveness of sexuality runs counter to the notion that human sexuality is naturally fixed and unchanging, the same for everyone everywhere. Matters are more complex. Sexuality is not a static "thing," but rather a dynamic process, constantly being reshaped and reassigned value and meaning amid conflicting social interests. According to Weeks, sexuality is "a peculiarly sensitive conductor of cultural influences,"[3] and because of its plasticity and chameleon-like ability to change shapes, it is seen differently by different peoples, cultures, and historical epochs. Its malleability also means that within a culture of injustice, sexuality becomes a "loaded" site of contested power and powerlessness, both a mirror for and a reinforcement of social injustice.

How is sexuality a structural problem, and what does it mean to say that eroticism becomes attached to injustice? Carter Heyward provides a useful analogy. A structure, she writes, is a "pattern of relational transactions that gives a society its particular shape." When a house has a structural problem, more is needed to fix it than new wallpaper or rearranging the furniture. Solving a structural problem requires digging down to the foundation of the edifice, uncovering any rot, and making basic repairs to put the building once again on sound footing. Then and only then, Heyward argues, "can we begin to reconstruct the house in such a way as to provide adequate, trustworthy space for all."[4] Similarly, a structural analysis of sexuality offers a critical assessment of its foundational assumptions and of the basic organization of the prevailing sexual system in order to determine the soundness of present arrangements and their adequacy for its "occupants."

The feminist insight that the personal is political makes a related claim. Personal life is shaped by social dynamics, including structured patterns of power and powerlessness. We live and love, or not, within societal arrangements. These same societal arrangements are reflected in, reinforced by, and sometimes challenged and transformed by the ways we live and love, or not. No sphere of personal life exists outside of or entirely divorced from the political, economic, and cultural forces that shape both the personal and the political. No autonomous, privatized space exists into which we can retreat and do our loving untouched by social realities. The world is with us always, including in our bedrooms. In an alienated world of injustice, sexuality itself will also be alienated. People are estranged *in their sexuality* from themselves and others, that is, not fully at home in their own bodies or in the company of other bodies.

The Needed Shift:
The Social Construction of Sexuality

A recent ecumenical survey of church studies about human sexuality offers this judgment: "The fact that the churches are so exercised on the subject suggests that God is calling us to rethink it."[5] But what is this "it" that requires rethinking? Of course, it is sexuality, but two different approaches—essentialism and constructionism—offer conflicting views on how to think about this elusive subject.

Sexual essentialism defines sex as a natural force, a fixed and unchanging essence that exists prior to and independent of sociocultural arrangements. Sex is a property belonging to individuals. It resides in their hormones, their psyches, or their genetic structures. Sex is "what comes naturally." Biological imperatives determine the "normal" course of things, what feels right, and what fits natural mandates. From an essentialist viewpoint, "sexuality has no history and no significant social determinants."[6] After all, essentialism asks, isn't sexuality what is *most* natural about humans and *least* susceptible to change?

Essentialists posit that when all goes according to plan, biological mandates give rise to a natural expression of sexual desire. In keeping with such naturalistic assumptions, heterosexuality is seen as natural and normal because it fits nature's anatomical design for male-female sexual intercourse and because it has a biologically functional purpose in reproducing the species. By this same logic, homosexuality is unnatural and abnormal. A troubling sleight of hand takes place, however, in some subtle shifts in language from "natural" to "normal" and the implied "normative." As sociologist Michael Kimmel suggests, "That which is *normative*—constructed and enforced by society through socialization of the young and through social sanctions against deviants—begins to appear as *normal*, that which is designed by nature."[7] The normative and the normal, however, in a statistical sense, are not necessarily the same. The normative, a product of moral discernment and deliberation, reflects a communal valuing of what is good, right, and fitting. Normative judgments, including those made about sexuality, are subject to challenge and revision. What *is* may be far off from what *ought* to be.

Essentialism falsely assumes that sexuality is the same for everyone, everywhere. Sexuality, however, is a more complex reality, more fluid and more amenable to cultural molding. In some cultures, people refrain from sex during the daytime while in other cultures sex is prohibited at night. Some societies are not at all concerned about when sex takes place but rather about where. Inside the house may be acceptable as long as it is not near the food supply, or sex may be permitted only outdoors.

Kissing is customary behavior in our culture, but some indigenous peoples in South America consider mouth-to-mouth kissing an offensive, even barbaric practice.[8] Therefore, what sexuality looks like and signifies varies from culture to culture. "Far from being the most natural element in social life, the most resistant to cultural moulding," Weeks argues, "[sexuality] is perhaps one of the most susceptible to organization."[9]

In contrast to essentialism, a social constructionist approach assumes that sexuality is constituted within, not apart from, society and history. Sexuality's purpose and meaning cannot be grasped by biology alone, but must be comprehended within its sociocultural context. This historical, contextualized approach puts the primary emphasis on analyzing sexuality *within* society and social relations. A significant ethical implication follows. If sexuality is socially constructed, then it is not a fixed and unalterable essence, but rather something susceptible to modification and transformation. Properly viewed, sexuality becomes a social and cultural issue as well as a personal concern. Furthermore, it makes sense to raise questions about sexuality in relation to injustice and the righting of distorted, harmful patterns of sexual interaction.

Historians trace shifting patterns of sexual practice and meanings in U.S. culture. From the start, the colonial period focused on reproductive sexuality within tightly regulated marriages. In the nineteenth century, however, the newly emergent bourgeoisie saw sexuality as a means to enhance personal intimacy within marriage while at the same time prescribing, within explicitly drawn race and class boundaries, privatized roles for women and public status for men. The twentieth century has once again shifted social meanings, this time toward the public depiction of sex. We witness a widespread commodification of sexuality and its commercialization, but also a strong cultural consensus that personal happiness is the primary goal of sexual relations.[10] Of course, change can also be traced on a personal as well as a cultural level. Over a lifetime, many if not most men and women experience changes in their sexual interests and practices. Few of us are the same sexually throughout our teens, twenties, forties, sixties, even eighties. For example, most of us who identify ourselves as gay, lesbian, or bisexual were raised by our families as if we were (and would always be) heterosexual. The shift in our own self-acknowledged identities, our disclosure to others, and our subsequent loss of heterosexual privilege, all have had a life-transforming effect on us. Yet other changes, including surviving a sexual assault or breaking with conventional gender role patterns, can mark equally significant turns in a person's journey. No matter what our gender or sexual orientation, the prevailing categories that delineate sexual identity and difference—male/female, heterosexual/homosexual, single/married—oversimplify the truth of our lives. The diversity of human sexualities is much more complex, dynamic, and interesting than such abstract categories typically manage to portray.

Social constructionists emphasize that sexuality is a dynamic and malleable process. Transformations in social practices and meaning occur, but these shifts take time and are not accomplished at will. Typically, the more significant changes are the result of sustained cultural struggle, which include a basic reorientation in conceptual frameworks. When paradigm shifts in social theory take place, they usually occur after protracted intellectual, moral, and political conflict between competing communities of interpretation. Advocates of a newer conceptual framework gain ascendancy sometimes because of the merits of their intellectual outlook, but often because they manage to convince more people. In a period when such a shift occurs, conflict between old and new paradigms intensifies. As ethicist Wilson Yates observes, "There is often uncertainty—the old paradigm which made us comfortable in its ability to make sense out of reality is breaking down and we experience ourselves living in a period of crisis, a time between the times when a secure way of understanding that particular reality eludes us." People are confronted by new, often unfamiliar ways of seeing and ordering their practices, and until any one particular pattern becomes dominant, "we are forced to explore a range of new possibilities whether we desire to do so or not."[11] When a shift finally occurs, the newer paradigm draws on insights from the earlier paradigm's way of organizing and making sense of reality, but these insights take on renewed meaning.

Cultural shifts in viewing human sexuality have occurred time and again during the modern period. For example, during the eighteenth century, as historian Thomas Laqueur has documented, the entire view of human sexual nature changed. The conventional view, firmly entrenched from the second century C.E., deployed a one-sex model of the human person. The female body was seen as an inferior version of the male body. Women were viewed anatomically as men turned "outside in." The vagina was assumed to function as an interiorized penis. Beginning in the early eighteenth century, this viewpoint was set aside in favor of a two-sex model. This alternative paradigm assumed that fundamental differences existed between males and females and that these differences were largely biological and anatomical in nature. This newer model of sex/gender dimorphism viewed men and women as "opposites," such that, as Laqueur writes, "not only are the sexes different, but they are different in every conceivable aspect of body and soul, in every physical and moral aspect." Science came to see this difference as one of kind and not of degree and as solidly lodged in nature.[12] However, the paradigm of two radically different, "opposite" sexes is as much a cultural construction as the earlier one-sex model.

Science reflects ideological interests and helps to promote them as legitimate. Historian Laqueur surmises that "no one was much interested in looking for evidence of two distinct sexes . . . until such differences became politically important." Biology was invoked to legitimate differentials in the social status of men and women and make these differentials appear natural rather than political in origin. Because science has the power to constitute and not merely observe difference, it is wise to question the ideological determination of any supposedly indisputable "facts" about human sexuality. As Laqueur concludes, "powerful prior notions of difference or sameness determine what one sees and reports about the body."[13]

Other established conventions about sexuality have either been questioned or abandoned altogether. The notion that men want sex and women want relationship functions as a truism within popular culture. This is a modern notion, however, and represents an inversion of pre-Enlightenment claims extending back to antiquity in which men were attributed with the capacity for friendship with men and women were associated with sensuality.[14] Culture rather than anatomy, at least in terms of the power of social norms and expectations, shapes destiny.

In another cultural shift, the view that homosexuality is a sickness or a mental and/or emotional disorder has been reevaluated by the profession that a century ago first created the concept of homosexuality and labeled it a disorder requiring treatment and cure. In 1973 the Board of Trustees of the American Psychiatric Association voted to remove homosexuality from its list of pathological disturbances. A similar resolution, adopted in early 1975 by the governing body of the American Psychological Association (APA), removed homosexuality from its list of mental disorders, adding that homosexuality by itself implies no impairment in judgment, character, stability, or social capacity. The latter organization has also urged mental health professionals to "take the lead in removing the stigma of mental illness . . . long associated with homosexual orientations."[15] In light of this critical renaming, social scientists have shifted their attention to investigating social prejudice against gay men, lesbian women, and bisexual persons. Homosexuality is no longer a "problem" to investigate or a disease to arrest or cure. Rather heterosexism, the institutionalizing of gay oppression, and homophobia, the fear and devaluing of same-sex eroticism, have become the primary focus of social, psychological, and ethical inquiry.[16] This reevaluation, however, did not take place without conflict or concerted struggle within the scientific community to redefine both sexual health and social deviance.

In this culture, all sexuality is categorized and labeled. Labeling is a social control mechanism that maintains power relations as given. One's sexual identity is presumed to be a fixed inner essence, publicly identifiable and expressive of a core truth about a person: He or she is either male or female, either heterosexual or homosexual. Most people assume, for example, that the label "homosexual" describes a master personality trait that governs the entirety of a person's thoughts, feelings, and actions. In accord with such labels, people expect those identified as "homosexual" to be maladjusted, unreliable, promiscuous, and perhaps even irreligious. Labeling establishes a deviant class of misfits whose activities are unacceptable and at odds with the rest of the social order.[17] At the same time, labeling creates a normative class, whose identity is based on negating others: A heterosexual is someone not homosexual. Social labeling encourages compliance with prevailing cultural norms and punishes gay and nongay persons alike from straying from male-dominant and female-subordinate patterns of social and sexual relating. Prescriptive labeling, coupled with a variety of sanctions, pressures people to accept, or at least not to overtly challenge, a heterosexual male norm as the idealized sexuality.

In yet another cultural shift, feminists identify a *women's* sexual revolution. Since the 1970s, women have developed a social discourse about sexuality based not on the authority of experts, but rather on the truth-claims of women's shared stories about their lives and struggles in a misogynous culture. Women's empowerment includes their erotic empowerment to claim their own right to sexual pleasure and fulfillment. This grassroots revolution, sparked by both lesbian and heterosexual women, has developed a new discourse about women's bodies and human sexuality. Women's experiences, desires, and needs, as well as women's own voices, receive central attention.[18] Some describe women's sexual revolution as a revolution of rising expectations. Feminist social theorist Barbara Ehrenreich observes, however, that "it is not that women simply [are having] more sex than they had in the past, but they [have begun] to transform the notion of heterosexual sex itself." Numbers of heterosexual women are no longer interested in a conventional model of genital sex that is male-centered and assumes female passivity. Women are exploring their own desires and capacities and their right to pleasure. Sexual interaction is being approached as a more open-ended encounter in which women are active and responsible in a new way for their own fulfillment. Sex itself is no longer defined as a "spontaneous outburst of (mostly male) passion but as an arena for negotiation where women [are] no longer the automatic losers."[19] Therefore, the feminist revolution has extended to the bedroom where many women (and some men) are struggling to displace patriarchal sex with sexual exchange that values women as sexual subjects.

A final example of a cultural shift is the moral revaluation of masturbation. In the early 1970s Karl Menninger observed that masturbation, regarded as the "great sin" in his youth, was now only rarely identified as wrong. Here, what was judged harmful in one generation was viewed as a benign, even commendable sexual practice by a subsequent generation. Contemporary theologians speak positively of masturbation as "that occasional gift through which we are graced to break through the sexual dualisms that beset and alienate us."[20] Such reappraisals of sexuality are not unique, but they are noteworthy nonetheless.

These examples illustrate that, in contrast to naturalistic assumptions about sexuality, a social-constructionist perspective expects change and variability through time and within diverse cultures and subcultures. Sexuality is a politically contested arena of human activity, open to the possibilities of transformation. It is therefore an area of human responsibility. Sexual persons are moral agents who, under adequate conditions of safety and freedom, can direct their sexual activity according to their value commitments. They are accountable for their choices even as they are being influenced by a cultural order that they, in turn, help to shape and reshape.

All social relations, including sexual relations, are subject to human agency, that is, to greater humanization or dehumanization. What happens depends, to some extent, on our personal conduct and moral choices, but also on sociocultural forces that bear upon and often limit people's actual choices. Any enhancement of sexual relations requires cultural and political alterations in the structures of power and meaning, because lasting change cannot be sustained only at the personal level. As Rosemary Radford Ruether observes, "The larger system still entraps us and limits our choices." Transforming the entire system of power and control is "the future that eludes us," Ruether concludes, not because such transformation is beyond our power as human, but rather "because it is not within our power as *individuals* or small groups. It demands the conversion of all, not only as individuals, but as a collective system."[21]

Scripting a Sexual Code

Examining how racism, sexism, and heterosexism affect sexuality is a necessary step toward discovering what must be done, personally and politically, to disentangle sexual desire and intimacy from injustice and oppression. All societies make arrangements to organize erotic life. Our society and our churches, in seeking to shape the character of human sexuality and to regulate its expression, are not unusual in this regard. Sex and sexuality, as discussed above, are never simply matters of "what comes naturally." Rather sexuality is encoded by the culture to reflect and reinforce that culture's values and interests. Such scripting or moral mapping gives sexuality its distinctive character within a particular cultural context.

To discover how sexual codes operate, consider the following exercise. Imagine two female friends meeting midday. Make a list of things they can do together in public that fit expectations of what is proper and respectable for two females. List, as well, activities that are improper for them.

Surely there would be no controversy if they were to shop together, play tennis, or share a meal in a restaurant, but is it proper for them to hold hands as they walk down the street or sit at the lunch table? Are they allowed to kiss? If so, what kind of kiss is permissible? When would it become suspect? Does it matter if they are related by blood or what their ages are? What difference does it make if they are from different racial groups? If one is the employer of the other?

Whether we are aware of it or not, our lives are circumscribed by sex/gender codes that regulate conduct in myriad, quite detailed ways. For example, these codes grant permission for women to engage in certain activities while proscribing others. These do's and don'ts can be specified in detail. Usually, over time, there comes to be some flexibility and degree of modification in the rules. With little effort we can detail the specifics of the cultural code that impinges on women's lives and regulates their relation to other women. We could also detail the operative code between women and men.

Continue this exercise, but now imagine two male friends meeting midday. Make a list of the things they can and cannot do together in public. Surely there would be no controversy if the two males were to shop together, play tennis, or share a meal in a restaurant, but is it proper for them to hold hands as they walk down the street or sit at the lunch table? May they kiss? If so, what kind of kiss is permissible? When would it become suspect? Does it matter if they are related by blood or what their ages are? What difference does it make if they are from different racial groups? If one is the employer of the other?

Again, such activities can be specified in considerable detail. Reasons can be enumerated why certain behaviors are permissible and others are not for two men, two boys, or a man and a boy. Without assuming that these rules are appropriate, we can recognize that definite rules are in force. Our social relations are shaped, to a significant degree, by a code of expectations we internalize and utilize daily to negotiate our way in the world as females or males.

Sociologists John Gagnon and William Simon have coined the term "sexual scripts" to refer to "the plans that people have in their heads for what they are doing and what they are going to do" as social actors.[22] In an open-ended process of socialization, people learn to read and comport themselves according to a certain script, much as actors learn their individual parts in a play. People, young and old, perform in the drama of sexual interaction and learn the risks and rewards of particular roles. Through observation, rehearsal, and performance, people become accustomed to what makes them feel fully "on stage" and sexy. They learn the proper moves and rituals of intimacy and what the right setting looks like, along with the right scenery, lights, and costumes. They learn what they and other performers should and should not do. Although the script is created, perfected, and then handed to us from an external source, like actors in a play we at times have some discretion, depending on our social status and power, to improvise and have the script reflect our own interpretation and more personal preferences. Although modifications may be allowed, sexual scripts are typically rigid within any given culture and are especially oppressive to nonconforming "performers." As Michael Kimmel observes, "This is why what is considered normal sexuality is so strikingly similar in any particular culture and why there are individual idiosyncratic variations on the normative theme."[23]

A structural analysis of the prevailing sexual system examines the cultural code about sexuality, investigates how social relations are regulated, and asks for what purposes erotic power is intended. Inequities in power and status are reflected in and reinforced by the dominant script. A liberating ethic of sexuality must therefore ask: How does this code represent "good sex"? Where, and by whom, are the lines drawn between acceptable and unacceptable behavior? Is respect shown for differences in sexual identity and expression? Does the code promote fairness? Are persons encouraged to feel at home in their bodies and to relate with respect to others? If not, what must be altered, and how?

Body Contempt and Disability as Moral Failure

Sexual injustice involves violation of the body (bodies) and denial of body right. In a culture of inequality, some persons, typically those with social power and privilege (white people, wealthy people, men, adults, the able-bodied), claim the right to control others (people of color, women, children, employees, the disabled) and to manage both their bodies and their lives. Racism, sexism, and heterosexism are habitual patterns of body violation or *body wrong* which are tolerated, in part, because of the contempt toward the body that persists in Western culture. Body respect, in contrast, is expressed by a community's commitment to body right, the entitlement of every person to his or her bodily integrity and self-direction. Every competent person should decide whether and how his or her body will be touched, used, and generally dealt with by others. Incompetent persons, whether because of age, circumstance, or condition and whether their incompetence is temporary or permanent, should also have their bodily integrity protected by responsible caregivers.

Respect for the body is foundational to moral life. People do not simply reside in their bodies or have bodies. Rather, we are our body-selves. Respect for the body undergirds respect for persons. "Our body-space," ethicist Beverly Harrison notes, "is literally the ground of our personhood and our means of communicating the power of our presence to and with others." Through physical touch, people have the means, at once tender and powerful, to communicate care, compassion, and mutual regard toward one another. Alternatively, through touch that seeks control and power over others, people can gesture disrespect, contempt, and disvalue toward themselves, others, and the world. As Harrison says, "How we deal with our own body-space and how we relate to others' provides a paradigm for all our moral relations to the world."[24]

Body *dis*respect characterizes racist, patriarchal social patterns of injustice. At its worst, disrespect becomes contemptuous and hateful toward the body and toward concrete, particular bodies. At a less harmful level, such disrespect renders people's bodies unimportant and their needs and yearnings either invisible or inconsequential. Body contempt and the "invisibilizing" of people are at the core of the oppression of disabled persons. Disability, like gender and race, is not a biological fact. It is a political-cultural construct based upon a biological reality. The cultural categorization of disability creates a class of persons who exist, if visible at all, only at the margins. Irving Kenneth Zola, in his first-person chronicle of living with disability, speaks of a process of oppression that renders people "invalids" or, with the accent slightly shifted, in-valid by denying them four central aspects of their humanity: their sexuality, their anger, their vulnerability, and their potentiality.

Persons with mental and physical limitations are often desexualized and thereby infantalized. To be rendered childlike is to be robbed of voice and power. As Zola recounts, sexual interest and activity are supposed to decline, if not disappear altogether, when illness appears. The return of sexual interest is taken as a sign of physical recovery. However, when someone is permanently disabled, "attractiveness and the ability and interest to engage in sex are often regarded as [permanently] impaired."[25] Restoration of sexual capacity and desire is presumed unlikely or even

unwelcome for the disabled, especially as long as sex is associated culturally with youthfulness and physical attractiveness.

The desexualizing of disabled persons reflects a cultural obsession with
perfect bodies and with the "normalcy" of penis-in-vagina sex. It not only
demonstrates ignorance about the sexual desires and capacities of disabled persons, but also communicates a fearful and punitive response to
them. As Zola comments, "Our society does not like to picture people
who are weak, sick, and even dying, having needs for sexual intimacy. It
is regarded as unseemly." Disabled persons, like other oppressed groups,
often internalize their oppression by denying or refusing to express a
desire for intimacy. They too may accept alienating cultural norms and
conclude that, as Zola writes, "in our condition of disablement or disfig-
urement, no one could (or should) find us sexually attractive."[26]

Philosopher Susan Wendell, herself a disabled person, argues that the
oppression of disabled people is linked to the more generalized cultural
oppression of the body and, more concretely, of physicality and the "real"
body. Our culture idealizes the body not only in terms of ideal physical
appearance, but also in terms of responsiveness and control of body functions. Because few persons measure up to the idealized standard of either
beauty or bodily performance, people generally feel alienated and distanced from their bodies.

Idealizing the body prevents able-bodied and disabled people alike
from identifying with and loving their real bodies. The endless and quite
futile quest for bodily perfection keeps people alienated because they can
at best only narrow the gap between the idealized body and their own for
a short period of time.[27] Moreover, because sexual desire is a primary
means of affirming one's personhood, the awareness of sexual desire (and
of being desirable) is intimately linked with securing a strong sense of
oneself as a moral agent with the capacity for self-direction. Repression of
sexual desire keeps people in doubt and uncertain about their own feelings and values. Moreover, when people lose touch with their feelings,
including their sexual feelings, they are likely to lose their interior com-
pass and become more readily susceptible to social control and exploitation. Therefore, claiming one's right to bodily self-determination and
holding onto one's own perception of what feels good, right, and pleasurable are key components in the lifelong moral formation of persons as
independent and conscientious moral agents.

The body is idealized in this culture, but something more is happening
that only heightens expectations of physical mastery and self-control.
People, especially those in subordinate roles, are expected to restrict their
desires and bodily needs. The quest for control places a particular onus on
disabled persons whose visible struggles with their bodies are seen moral-

istically as failure to exercise self-control. Even though able-bodied persons also experience degrees of body impairment during their lifetime, they seldom identify with disabled persons or fully appreciate their coping strengths. The cultural preoccupation with bodily perfection oppresses disabled persons, but also alienates all persons from their experiences of embodiment and heightens their fear of bodily change.

Disabled persons, culturally designated as the Other, symbolize a dreaded loss of body control, diminished autonomy, and death, all things that people in a body- and death-denying culture seek to evade. Ynestra King, whose childhood polio created for her a mild but noticeable mobility restriction, argues that visibly disabled persons are scapegoats for the pervasive resentment in this culture toward any limitation on physical, organic life. "The ostracization, marginalization, and distorted response to disability are not simply issues of prejudice and denial of civil rights," she argues. "They reflect attitudes toward bodily life, an unease in the human skin, an inability to cope with contingency, ambiguity, flux, finitude, and death."[28] If we would listen to those with physical, mental, or emotional limitation and learn from them about resisting the culturally idealized body, Susan Wendell suggests "we would have less fear of the negative body, less fear of our own weakness and 'imperfections', and of our inevitable deterioration and death."[29]

Because our culture prizes radical self-sufficiency, fears death, and infantalizes those who exhibit human vulnerability (all of us eventually), there is little tolerance for a disabled person's lack of independence or persistent need to rely upon the help of others. Cultural myths of radical autonomy reinforce the oppression of the disabled. The disabled represent those who have not managed to control the neediness of their bodies. Therefore they appear not only as different, but as wrong. As King concludes, "To need help is to feel humiliated, to have failed," especially in the United States, "because our heroes are dynamic overcomers of adversity, and there is an inevitable cultural contempt for weakness." The hatred of the disabled, she argues, is rooted in their lack of autonomy, along with their visible embeddedness in nature and the body.[30] Here we face a serious moral problem. Instead of perpetuating the ancient yet persistent attitude that physical (and mental) disability is a sign of sin and moral failure, perhaps we should regard disability sacramentally. Would it not be fairer and more realistic to affirm disability as an "outward and visible sign" of the human condition? A fragile and complex web of interconnections sustains our living, eases our dying, and makes possible a community of both memory and hope. We live in this world only as vulnerable, interdependent creatures, and our mutual dependency is the norm, not the aberration.

Fixation with control of the body is intimately connected to the contempt for the disabled. If, as Susan Wendell claims, "suffering caused by the body, and the inability to control the body, are despised, pitied, and above all, feared," this fear is socially managed by able-bodied persons who project onto persons with disabilities what they fear and reject in themselves. The disabled represent, at a safe distance, the failure of the negative, nonnormative body. While both able-bodied and disabled persons are capable of projection and objectification, this process is seldom a symmetrical one. The disabled population lacks the social power to institutionalize itself as the normative paradigm of humanity. It simply does not have the political means to remake the world to fit its needs or reflect its own experiences.[31]

The culturally normative able-bodied paradigm, with its contempt for body weakness and vulnerability, penalizes disabled persons in particular, but diminishes everyone's humanity. It does this first, by fostering an illusory bodily perfection and second, by fostering a quest for radical independence from the social web of life. The truth of our lives, however, is that we live in, and because of, our bodies. We live because of, not in spite of, our embodied connections with and dependence on other bodies. From birth onward, we utterly depend upon flesh-and-blood care and how well our communities provide ongoing structures of support. Our shared vulnerability establishes our common humanity and also makes securing body right for all people a matter of moral urgency.

White Racism's
Embodied Logic of Supremacy

The social construction of sexuality cannot be understood apart from racism and the cultural construction of white racial supremacy. The cultural obsession with an idealized body is an obsession to maintain the normativity of (adult) white men and their right to control others. In this culture affluent white men are assigned the right of access to women, children, and nonwhite men, as well as the right to manage their bodies, including their productive and reproductive labor. Socially powerful men are expected to control the lives of social inferiors.

In this culture everyone receives moral instruction about how social domination is justified by human differences, that is, by measurable deviations from the white, affluent male norm. When human differences are ranked hierarchically and naturalized, people see differences as markers of dominant or subordinate status. They learn to fear that those with more power will harm them or that those with less power will take away their privileges. Some fear is of course warranted, especially among women and people of color, because of rape, lynchings, and other forms of social control. This fear, however, can also be exaggerated and used to discourage people from banding together across their differences to challenge abuses of power and to promote safety and mutual respect as community norms. Because difference is routinely associated with domination, a generalized fear is promoted *not of domination, but of difference itself*. This fear keeps the socially marginalized in line and all people mistrustful of efforts to alter power dynamics.[32]

Fear, suspicion, and intolerance are marks of a social order in which sexism, racism, and other injustices teach the devaluing of difference. Therefore, gaining awareness of and mounting resistance to racist patriarchal standards of superiority and inferiority is a means of transcending fear and also enlarging human loving. Race and sex/gender oppression constrict people's natural affections to a closed social circle. In a racist culture, people rarely exhibit what sociologist Patricia Hill Collins calls a "big love." Big loving depends on trust that men can love and truly value women, that whites can see blacks as fully human, and that men-loving-men and women-loving-women can be respected as dignified members of the community. In the midst of multiple oppressions, however, our affective knowledge of our common humanity becomes distorted. The capacity to identify with each other and delight in our diversity "must be distorted on the emotional level of the erotic," Collins suggests, "in order for oppressive systems to endure."[33] Our fear of others lodges in our bodies, not merely in our heads. Basic human feelings of trust, respect, and playful curiosity about diversity have been corrupted, and our fellow-feeling has been diminished.

Supremacist models of sexuality promote an ethic of alienation, possession, and control. Injustices, including sexism and racism, are eroticized, so that what stirs many people is not a passion for justice as right-relatedness and mutual regard, but rather a perverse desire to exercise power over someone else, especially someone "not their kind," or alternately, a felt need to be put down and kept in one's place of inferiority. In a culture of inequality, the sexual problematic, as Beverly Harrison contends, is fear of genuine intimacy and mutuality among social equals.[34]

Race itself is not a natural, objective category for dividing groups or assigning differentials of power and status, but rather a political and cultural category, institutionalized in systemic patterns of ownership and control of one group by another. In the words of Audre Lorde, racism institutionalizes and culturally represents "the belief in the inherent superiority of one race over all others and thereby the right to dominance."[35] In a racist society, encountering race does not mean encountering difference within social relations of equality, shared power, and mutual respect, but rather within long-standing patterns of inequality, disrespect, and fear. White supremacy has crafted a social world of permanent race inequality, justified by naturalistic assumptions that white-skinned persons differ from persons of color in those moral and physical aspects that supposedly legitimize white mastery and control. Furthermore, white supremacy is a major component of the social construction of sexuality, and racist ideology is tightly intertwined with sex-negativity. White racism assumes that sexuality differentiates Euro-Americans from African Americans. The sexuality of black people is seen as chaotic, a power outside white control, and therefore something both deviant and mesmerizing. As Cornel West points out, "Americans are obsessed with sex and fearful of black sexuality."[36]

Black sexuality is subject to relentless stereotyping and projections of white fear onto black bodies. Dominant white culture or, more accurately, white racial narcissism assigns permanent negative value to the color black. Womanist theologian Delores Williams observes that white culture "considers black frightening, dangerous and/or repulsive—especially when this is the color of human bodies."[37] As I have already noted, the human body is a powerful signifier, and amplifier, of social fears and ideological conflicts. Black bodies, something both fearful and fascinating in the dominant culture, are a highly visible, hotly contested site of ideological claims. Moreover, white fear of and suspicion toward black sexuality gives white racism an energy and its edge. This fear, Cornel West suggests, is based on the degradation of black bodies and on white determination to control them.[38] Similarly, Williams cites the exploitation of black women under slavery and the demands made that slave women surrender their bodies to their owners. Black women's sexual labor, including their nurturing capacities as mothers and as community leaders, was made available to whatever powerful white persons, male or female, demanded their submission. Black women were, therefore, "bound to a system that had no respect for their bodies, their dignities or their motherhood, except as it was put to the service of securing the well-being of ruling-class families."[39] In this culture white supremacy has been the primary obstacle to securing body right for women and men of color.

Racism and sexuality have long intersected in white Western culture. Beginning in the seventeenth century, Europeans drew on racial and sexual ideology to differentiate themselves from indigenous peoples. They justified destruction of local cultures and appropriation of their land by labeling others as sexually and morally inferior. In the nineteenth century, sexuality continued to serve as an instrument of white dominance. White people viewed themselves as rational and civilized and others, especially blacks and Native peoples, as irrational and savage. As propertied white men struggled during times of economic dislocation and cultural flux, they invested in a morality of (white) female purity which forced "their" women and children into the "safe haven" of the privatized home. "Stereotypes of immoral women of other races," historians John D'Emilio and Estelle Freedman argue, only "contributed to the belief in white superiority" and to the avoidance of racial amalgamation because of the fear that "it would debase whites to the status of other races."[40] Sexual rule making rigidified as white males experienced moral panic in response to increasing cultural instability.

Throughout the United States and elsewhere, affluent white men have promulgated the moral superiority of white family practices and sexual customs. At the same time, supremacist attitudes justified their taking control of others and their sexual exploitation of women of color, including Native, Mexican, African, and African-American women. The sexual ideology of "true womanhood" pedestalized (and disempowered) white women as spiritually superior to men and reduced their social role to dutiful wives and mothers. In contrast, women from subjugated groups were identified with sensuality and the body, an identification white women were not allowed to possess. Nonwhite and poor women were de-spiritualized and seen as bound to the body and animalistic. White men objectified black women and shamelessly exploited them, sexually and economically. With the abolition of slavery, protecting white women's moral superiority became the justification for white men's intimidation of the black community through rape, castration, and lynchings. Then and now, violence imposed through sex was an effective means of social control for maintaining a white supremacist social order.

Three examples will illustrate how sexualized racism distorts human relationality. First, myths about sexual violence convey racist assumptions. Although most rapes are *intraracial*, that is, the victimizer belongs to the victim's own racial group, the social myth persists that most white woman are raped by black men. This belief teaches fear between whites and blacks. As Marie Fortune explains, it also "distract[s] white women from realizing that their most likely assailant will be a white man."[41] Furthermore, white race-supremacy compounds the injustice of sexual assault and coercion. When women of color are raped, they are seen as naturally promiscuous, less worthy of protection, and deserving what they get. Racism also distorts the responses to victimizers. "If the offender is a white male," Fortune observes, "the assumption is that he can take what he wants. If the offender is a male of color, it's assumed that 'that's the way those people behave normally.' "[42] In addition, men of color are frequently scapegoats for other men's sexual violence. Among incarcerated rapists, a disproportionately high number are men of color convicted of sexual assaults. Among these, a high number receive the most severe sentences, including capital punishment. White men, as a group, run a small risk of ever being prosecuted in the first place.[43] "The myth of the Black rapist," as Angela Davis notes, "renders people oblivious to the realities of rape."[44] Rape is a crime occurring most frequently *within* social groupings and, statistically, remains predominantly a white male crime against white women.

A second illustration of the intersection of racism and body hate is found in the United States health care system. Bodily integrity and vulnerability are particularly acute matters during illness. Whatever is deficient, however, about the health care system is worse for those who are female and nonwhite. African Americans report being treated like animals by everyone from orderlies to physicians.

> Since blacks are assumed to be less sensitive than white patients, they get less privacy. Since blacks are assumed to be more ignorant than whites, they get less by way of explanation of what is happening to them. And since they are assumed to be irresponsible and forgetful, they are more likely to be given a drastic, one-shot treatment, instead of a prolonged regimen of drugs, or a restricted diet.[45]

Racism is also evident in the training of interns at a dental clinic, whose policy as late as the mid-1970s was not to use anesthesia when operating on black patients. Interns learned how deep to drill by observing the pain response of their nonanesthetized patients. Because of institutionalized racism, blacks were treated as "teaching material." Why use anesthesia on a teaching device? "Anesthesia would deaden the pain and dull the intern's learning experience."[46] White supremacy subjects black bodies to abuse, neglect, and exploitation and renders them invisible or unworthy of respect and care.

A third illustration shows how racism diminishes black self-esteem and the ability to love black bodies. White racism rests on the devaluing of dark-skinned persons and their bodies. Through an imperial gaze, what bell hooks describes as "the look that seeks to dominate, subjugate, and colonize,"[47] standards of beauty are established that overvalue whiteness and devalue blackness. Euro-American definitions of aesthetic value, captured in the white male gaze, are made normative. People of color are defined and graded in relation to white ideals. With the imposition of alien standards, African Americans are taught self-hatred and body alienation. As Cornel West asserts, "much of black self-hatred and self-contempt has to do with the refusal of many black Americans to love their own bodies—especially their black noses, hips, lips, and hair."[48]

Black self-loathing is a legacy of institutionalized white supremacy. It instructs blacks, through fear and exploitation, that their lives are less worthy and that their personhood is deficient. The ongoing challenge for black people is to resist white cultural imperialism and stop viewing themselves through white lenses. "Black people will never value themselves," West concludes, "as long as they subscribe to a standard of valuation that devalues them."[49]

Racist patriarchy renders all women objects for male gazing and control, but all women are not treated the same. The objectification of black women on the slave auction block, disrobed and enchained objects for public display, may well be the historical precursor of the pornographic representation of the female body as an object of desire and possession by the detached male observer. However, as Patricia Hill Collins points out, racism creates a difference in how male pornography portrays various women. White women are turned into objects, but black women are turned into animals. "Race," Collins argues, "becomes the distinguishing feature in determining the type of objectification women will encounter."[50] Black women are caricatured as over-sexualized, promiscuous, and always "ready for sale," while white women are more often desexualized and caricatured as powerless, infantile, and socially compliant. All women experience sexist oppression, but white racism creates real differences in gender and sexual oppression. "Domination may be either cruel and exploitative with no affection," Collins notes, "or may be exploitative yet coexist with affection."[51] Whether women are treated as wild animals or as domesticated pets depends, to a great extent, on racist norms.

White supremacist ideology is awash with, and serves to maintain, sexist and sex-negative assumptions that deny body right to socially disenfranchised people, especially women of color. It also teaches socially powerful men, especially affluent white men, that they are entitled to control the bodies of others. Body contempt and body control are intimately bound up with racism and also, we shall next consider, with sexism and heterosexism.

Patriarchal Sex as Gender Control

In a patriarchal culture the kind of sex scripted as normative is patriarchal sex.[52] Heterosexual pornography discloses the essential element of a patriarchal construction of human sexuality: male ownership of women and children. Patriarchal ideology naturalizes these relations and asserts that women need men, as children need adults, to discipline and manage their lives—for their own good. As writer and profeminist activist John

Stoltenberg explains, patriarchal culture "romanticizes, spiritualizes, emotionalizes, and psychologizes the right of men to own women and children as property." At the same time, it "tends to obscure the violence in those structures of human relationship that are essentially structures of possession, as of inanimate objects."[53]

Historically, patriarchy has meant male rule in the family, as well as in the polis, where only male heads of household could be citizens. Racism, classism, heterosexism, and other structures of injustice, however, disempower some men and place them under the supervision of more powerful males. Therefore, the primary beneficiaries of male gender supremacy are white, property-owning men whose entitlement to control others, including less powerful men, is justified by appeals to nature and religion.

Our culture is preoccupied with gender or, more precisely, with maintaining male gender supremacy. The gender of the person to whom one is erotically attracted, along with their race and class identity, receives enormous weight. In fact, the gender of one's love-object choice, to use social scientific jargon, is the standard by which persons are judged normal or not. But why this intense interest in gender for determining the proper ordering of sexual relations?

A patriarchal ethic grants permission only for those erotic exchanges "in private" that uphold the gendered social hierarchy of male dominance. All social relations, including sexual relations, are restricted according to gender, race, and class, but gender ordering is particularly effective in personalizing social alienation. Permission is granted only for sex between a man and a woman within the institution of a male-dominant marriage or ownership pattern. Permission may also be given to sexually active single heterosexuals as long as they are, or appear to be, on their way to marriage. A double standard, however, encourages men to gain sexual access to any woman they can. A woman not attached to a man is vulnerable, but so is a woman attached to a less powerful man, especially a poor woman or a woman of color. The patriarchal code values a hierarchical social ordering between unequals. Patriarchy's ethic is an ethic of gender control.

Patriarchal sex is constructed on two assumptions: gender inequality and male control of women's bodies and their lives. Men are socialized to expect power over women as an entitlement. They often feel uncomfortable when not exercising that control. Staying in control requires keeping a manly distance from others (being cool and detached) and controlling feeling, especially feelings of remorse for trampling upon the humanity of others. Women, on the other hand, are socialized to accept powerlessness and social dependency as something right for them. Under patriarchy, a well-adjusted woman welcomes being under a man's direction. His control makes her feel more like a real woman and makes him feel more like a real man.

In this patriarchal organization of sexuality, the eroticization of dominant/subordinate gender relations means that erotic desire is sparked by gender inequities as so-called opposites "attract." Status inequalities turn many people on. Mutual respect or sharing power is not considered very sexy. Until the scope of this moral dilemma is grasped, however, the human costs inflicted by the cultural crisis of sexuality will never be accurately calculated. Patriarchal sex thrives on conquest and surrender, on winning control over another (or being placed under someone else's control). The popularity of romance novels in the U.S. mass market illustrates the influence of this cultural image of sexual intimacy. These novels suggest that women "really, really" enjoy, even secretly desire, being swept away and overwhelmed by a man who takes charge and "has his way with her," as Rhett Butler did with Scarlett O'Hara in *Gone with the Wind*. Because overpowering women is, in fact, the prevailing cultural pattern for heterosexual relations, clear boundaries between what constitutes sexual intimacy, on the one hand, and sexual violence, on the other, are not readily discernible in a patriarchal culture. Male sexuality is presented as predatory, female sexuality as masochistic.[54] Such alienated gender/sex roles may be complementary, but they are hardly liberating for women or men. As Karen Lebacqz argues, both men and women may question whether in overpowering a woman, a man is raping her or simply "being a man," in his eyes and perhaps also in hers.[55] For some people, sexuality and violence/violation are so intertwined that they can hardly be differentiated.

Sexuality conditioned by male gender supremacy eroticizes power inequalities. Relations of domination and subordination become erotically titillating. Many heterosexual men are turned on by female powerlessness and turned off by strong, assertive female partners. Through such skewed eroticism, people accept *in their bodies*, as well as in their psyches, that sexism is right and natural, the "way things are," and that male gender supremacy feels good. Gender injustice even seems pleasurable, a source of delight rather than the moral offense it is. Male gender supremacy feels right to many people because it exists within a wider cultural matrix that teaches people to be comfortable with, and to normalize, human indignities and a variety of social oppressions.

To understand how oppression distorts human intimacy, consider what John Stoltenberg names as the nexus of eroticism and ethics or dialectic between feeling good and doing right. Ethics involves loyalty to values and the commitment to do right. Eroticism involves the embodiment of sensation and feeling. In their lovemaking, people shape their moral character and, literally, embody their values as moral agents. In patriarchy, men and women learn the importance of doing right according to patriarchal norms and values. There are rewards for conforming, as well as sanctions for not conforming, to gender expectations of what the "right male thing" and the "right female thing" are in the public arena and in the bedroom. An embodied interplay or sensory hookup between feeling and doing conveys a powerful message. Turning on erotically requires compliance with patriarchal norms.

An intimate, somatized connection links personal identity with maintenance of the cultural system. Stoltenberg writes, "In no arena of human activity are people more loyal to that sex-specific ethics than in transactions involving overt genital stimulation."[56] When people have sex, they typically act in conformity with patriarchal gender norms. Jeffrey Weeks argues similarly that "modern culture has assumed an intimate connection between the fact of being biologically male or female (that is, having appropriate sex organs and reproductive potentialities) and the correct form of erotic behaviour (usually genital intercourse between men and women)."[57] The term "sex" conveys this link by referring both to a category of persons and to an act. The culture links identity and practice in a way that reinforces patriarchal gender formation.

When many men have sex, the power and control they feel in the when, the how, and the "to whom" they feel sexual are all matters that confirm, or fail to confirm, their socially constructed, gendered identity as men. Patriarchal sex reinforces men's deeply felt, somatized sense of being social superiors. The patriarchal sexual script focuses, for example, on the male's ability to perform sexually (genitally) and thereby experience himself as a real man. Being manly means "to be regarded by his partner as having no tactile, visual, behavioral, or emotional resemblance to a *not*-male, a female." Stoltenberg even speculates that many people's experience of sexual tension may be due to a socially induced gender anxiety about whether they are "behaving within the ethical parameters of what is wrong or right conduct for their putative sexual identities." Patriarchal sex seeks confirmation that one is "male enough" or "female enough." That self-knowledge, and self-doubt, becomes registered in one's body, the lived-in space through which people encounter the world and each other.[58]

As patriarchal constructions take hold in the body, power as sexualized domination becomes extremely effective, Patricia Hill Collins hypothesizes, "precisely because it is felt and not conceptualized."[59] Patriarchy is acquired at the feeling, somatic level of our being. Male gender supremacy is sensed, rather than simply thought about, through actions giving rise to feelings of being a "real man," in charge and entitled to deference from females and other social subordinates. Whatever actions validate male gender supremacy are valued and selected because they produce the desired feeling of belonging to the sex class of men. In fact, "most men's sexuality is tied up with gender-actualizing—with feeling like a real man. . . ."[60] Men who rape express vividly this patriarchal logic. Research shows that rapists rely on coercive sex to reinforce their sense of being manly. One man declared, "Forced sex is great, [I believed] I wouldn't get caught, and, besides, women love it." Another man identified how he benefited from taking possession of another person: "Rape was the ability to have sex without caring about the woman's response. I was totally dominant."[61] Patriarchal sex eroticizes domination as a man's rightful due.

There is a correlation between what happens in the social order in terms of race, gender, and other forms of oppression, and what happens in our bedrooms. As I discussed earlier, sex is culturally scripted to promote a certain patterning of social relations. Some men and women, forever creative and free-spirited, try to rewrite the script. They improvise as best they can, but the political becomes personalized insofar as parties are conditioned by patriarchal norms. When we act sexually, our actions and the meanings we attach to them confirm our gendered identities, our race status, and our relative privilege or disadvantage. In a gender and race-preoccupied social order, sex offers a means to confirm our gender and race identities. Engaging in the "right" kind of sex with the "right" kind of person becomes a proof of our authenticity as "real" men or "real" women with certain social standing and privilege (or lack thereof).

Sociologist Michael Kimmel summarizes this interplay of identity and social structure by saying that "we construct a sexuality through gender, and we confirm gender through sexual behavior." He illustrates his point by examining what happens to many men when they experience common sexual problems, such as erectile dysfunction, premature ejaculation, or low sexual interest. Men will, tellingly, define their problem in gender rather than sexual terms. For example, they will interpret their trouble as a performance problem, a failure of not being "good enough" men. Men with low sexual interest will complain that they "simply don't feel like" real men. In compliance with the male supremacist script, a man may be concerned less about sexual pleasure and more with his validation as a properly gendered male. "Sexual performance," Kimmel concludes, "is a confirmation of gender scripts."[62]

Sexuality conditioned by male gender supremacy eroticizes power inequalities, bolsters male control, and increases people's comfort level with oppression. Supremacist sexuality conditions people to respond sexually to persons of the "right" gender, but also to the "right" race and class. Only persons from the right social status are marriageable, that is, suitable as partners because they match dominant cultural norms. Social norms are violated, for example, when a man has sex with another man, but only mildly so if he is "discreet" enough to maintain patriarchal appearances and can reassure others (and perhaps himself) that nothing has really changed because of his wayward behavior. By keeping sex with another man a "private" matter, he offers no threat to racist patriarchal norms. His offense becomes much greater, and the penalties stronger, when he shows genuine affection and care for other men, some of whom he may also desire to touch sexually. Patriarchal taboo is directed not at infringing upon men's sexual activity, but rather at preventing men's love for, and intimacy with, persons of the "wrong" gender, race, and class.[63]

Heterosexism, the Linchpin of Control

A related dynamic further entrenches gender injustice. Heterosexism, the structural dynamic of antigay and antilesbian oppression, grants moral value to heterosexuality alone and presumes that everyone should be heterosexual. Homophobia is the fear of homosexuals, but also the fear of loving someone of the same sex and of being gay or queer oneself—that is, someone who loves others who are the same as and equal to themselves. Homophobia is the feeling-signal that heterosexism is operative. Heterosexism reinforces sexism by applying pressure, including violence when necessary, to ensure that people play their proper dominant/subordinate gender roles. Gay-bashers, like batterers and rapists, are moral enforcers of the patriarchal code.

Heterosexism guarantees compliance with dominant/subordinate gender dynamics. In this culture, people are subject not only to threats of heterosexist violence, but often feel pain, fear, and shame if they experience homoerotic desire. Body shame is a cost gay men and lesbian women pay as "abnormal" lovers of forbidden body selves. Deviance from sexism is punished. Gay and nongay persons alike are coerced to conform to male gender supremacy in the family and elsewhere. Heterosexism labels any departure from normative heterosexuality unnatural, disordered, and subversive. Homosexuality is out of (patriarchal) order because it challenges the normativity and inevitability of dominant/subordinate gender roles. If compulsory heterosexuality and its correlate—compulsory coupling—weaken, other forms of social oppression also weaken.

Male gender supremacy discourages any desire for mutual love. Men are not to love and respect women as their equals, but rather to desire being on top of them. The eroticized link between patriarchal sex and male gender identity keeps many men stuck in place, sweating it out and doing their duty to keep women in their subordinate place. All the while, a heterosexist ethic insists that real men enjoy—take pleasure in—dominating women. By restricting erotic exchange to relations of domination, patriarchy socializes men to desire only heterosexual sex as real, but also to enjoy a general "lording over" women and less powerful males. Dominating others, however, is dehumanizing and morally alienating. Men must be kept loyal to the cause. Therefore, strong cultural sanctions are kept ready at hand, including violence and threats of violence, to intimidate men from disengaging from the male hierarchical game. Any man not properly performing his dominant role with women is derided as a sissy, a queer, or simply a failed man, "little better than a woman." Similarly, a strong, self-respecting, and assertive woman may be labelled a "man-hater" or assumed to be lesbian. Such labelling has nothing to do with sexual orientation or erotic preference. Rather, the label functions as a social control mechanism to keep her fearful and bound to her socially prescribed inferiority. Patriarchal sex teaches women to be available to serve others, especially men, and to limit their moral viewpoint by taking others, not themselves, into account. According to patriarchal logic, normal women enjoy being sexually submissive and socially compliant; normal men enjoy being dominant and sexually aggressive.

Heterosexism reinforces gender injustice and undergirds all other forms of dominant/subordinate relations. Heterosexism and homophobia pollute the channels of sexual intimacy on which people depend for open and trustworthy communication. Patriarchal sex diminishes our common well-being as males and females and as heterosexual, homosexual, and bisexual persons. In the midst of this oppressive social structure, we can easily lose our authentic humanity. We can find ourselves mistaking mere body sensations for the delight of sensuous touch born of mutual respect. We may yearn for, but cannot easily establish, life-enhancing connections, person to person. Estranged from each other, we struggle to make those emotional, cognitive, physical, and spiritual connections with one another that alone make life joyful and worth living.

A Racist Patriarchal Legacy of Fear and Control

A racist patriarchal construction of sexuality gives rise to a fearful, defensive sexual ethic. Erotic energy is viewed as an alien, negative force impinging from the outside on the "real" self and threatening reason and order. When viewed this way, sexuality becomes a problem that individuals and society must manage, by external controls if necessary. The underlying presumption is that sex is guilty until proven innocent. The burden of proof is placed on sex to show that it can be ethically justified. Typically, sex is something officially tolerated as a necessary evil. Sex is redeemable only by serving a good end outside itself, either procreation or the restraint of lust.

In the dominant scheme, sex is imagined as an unequal social relation between a social superior (male) and a social inferior (female). It ceases to be about either love or mutual pleasure between willing partners. Sex is instrumentalized as a control dynamic between a powerful subject and "his" submissive object. Traditional Christian sexual ethics, by perpetuating an ethic of male ownership of female bodies, differentiates "good" and "bad" sex by the particular use men make of women. Either the man uses the woman rightly for procreation or wrongly for indulgent, selfish pleasure.[64] Sex is not viewed as mutually desired intimacy between peers.

Unless this patriarchal framework of control is criticized, sexual relations, forever defined as exclusively heterosexual, are morally imagined as relations of domination. The male has the right to initiate, direct, and evaluate the interaction. His pleasure is his focus as well as hers. Sexual exchange maintains one person's power over another.

In the patriarchal imagination, sex is something one person "does to" another by imposing upon or taking from her (or him). Patriarchal sex is alienated sex. It distances men and women from their own bodies and from each other. Not surprisingly, many people express genuine confusion about the difference between sexual intimacy and violence.[65] In fact, sexual touching is often indistinguishable from violations of personhood. Many women, subject to lifelong sexual objectification, speak of their struggle to be "good girls" by attending to men's needs. They report only limited knowledge of their own sexual desires and capacities. Alienated from their bodies and lacking encouragement to pursue their own pleasure *as sexual subjects*, they have few clues about what feels genuinely good and right for them.

The church often plays a parental role by granting permission for sex and maintaining the rules about what is permissible. This arrangement fosters moral minimalism (what is forbidden, and how to avoid it?) and dependency (what does God, church, or this external authority define as right, and how can I stay in their good graces?). One denominational staff person lamented that when her denomination engaged in a major study of sexuality, there were "only two sentences of a social statement that most people [were] really interested in." They were, first, whether sex outside marriage is permissible and, second, whether same-sex genital sexual expression is sinful. Explaining moral complexities or offering nuanced ethical arguments, she wrote, is "considered by many to be beside the point," simply "high-fallutin attempts of elites to 'liberalize' the church's positions."[66]

Patriarchal Christianity regards absolute, exceptionless rules as the essence of morality. Many people feel guilty if they exercise any measure of sexual freedom or engage even in mild sexual experimentation, including learning through masturbation about one's body and its capacities for pleasure. By indulging in moralisms about sex, church people shy away from, and frequently miss altogether, critical insights that can emerge only from self-reflection about one's life in dialogue with others. That dialogue, of course, becomes richer when conducted by those facing quite different choices and responsibilities. Within patriarchal Christianity, however, the message from pulpits and pews is "give us the prohibitions or permissions—preferably straight from the Bible—not any convoluted discussions or rationalizations."[67]

Patriarchal Christianity promulgates an ethic of control. Taboos are offered instead of informed, self-critical ethical reflection. Patriarchal Christianity thereby encourages both clergy and laity alike to respond to sexuality in largely fear-based, reactive ways. Clergy bear a particular responsibility, however, for perpetuating the ignorance and denial of the laity about sexuality and sexual injustice. Church leaders, when trained in the school of patriarchal control, show little interest in challenging prevailing moral convention, no matter how dehumanizing or oppressive, and rarely demonstrate the courage necessary to work through controversial issues, especially when it relates to sex. That remains the sad truth even though, as William Sloane Coffin acknowledges, "most people in the pews are far more prepared for painful truths than we [clergy] give them credit for."[68]

In this culture sex appears to be an open topic, but it is not talked about freely or easily anywhere. Many try to keep sexuality and erotic energy safely tucked away within narrowly prescribed limits, officially contained in heterosexual marriage and supposedly placed out of the reach of the young and unmarried. Something quite different, however, is taking place.

What is denied, restricted, and repressed is erupting all over the place in the form of explicitly commercialized, commodified sexuality, paraded out in public in order to manipulate people's desires and sell merchandise. In this sense, sex is everywhere, but not in ways that empower most people's self-confidence or skills as self-directing moral agents. Surveys show that older and younger adults alike lack accurate information about sexuality. Whatever knowledge they acquire they gain indirectly, without clear comprehension of its significance for their lives.[69] Sexuality continues to be shrouded by ignorance, fear, and shame. As Larry Uhrig, a pastor and gay man, observes, "Growing up without a forum to question or channels to explore one's emerging sexual identity has inhibited and debilitated the health and maturation process of all people." Growing up as gay, lesbian, or bisexual only adds "layer after layer of guilt and obstacles to healthy sexual adjustment."[70]

In its patriarchal mode, therefore, sexual discourse is not about self-knowledge, intimacy, and the pleasures of embodied sensuality. It is about fear, control, and the containment of sexual desire, as well as its commodification. In chapter 3, I examine resources for resisting injustice and for developing a more liberating moral tradition that might bring justice and pleasure together as intimate partners for the common good.

3

Locating Resources
for a Liberating Ethic

The appropriate response to injustice
is outrage and protest—not polite dialogue.[1]
—John Fortunato

The vocation of progressive people is to oppose whatever blocks human well-being, diminishes communal life, or jeopardizes the earth's integrity, and to work toward justice as communal and cosmic right relation. Matters are complicated, however, for religious people seeking relief from sexual injustice. Christian tradition, including scripture and church teaching, has had a heavy hand in shaping the prevailing body-denying, sex-negative paradigm of human sexuality. One historian sums up matters by saying, "Traditional western Christianity [has been] a sex negative religion, regarding sex as necessary for procreation, but emphasizing celibacy as the ideal."[2] This religious tradition has shown antipathy and, at times, outright hostility toward sexuality.

What does this negative legacy imply for framing a liberating ethic of sexuality? A major consequence is the absence of a reliable, usable tradition of theological and ethical wisdom about sexuality that could guide us toward erotic justice. Insofar as traditional teachings about sexuality are a hindrance, they must be criticized and transformed. Those seeking sexual justice, within and outside the church, must be prepared to undertake what feminist theologian Carter Heyward calls a "journey without maps."[3]

In this chapter I begin by examining how Christianity has been a powerful weapon compounding people's suffering. This reality, however, must be held in tension with another truth about Christianity. Christian tradition for some women, gay men, and other marginalized persons has been a source of strength and encouragement for resisting oppression. If Christianity is to provide consistent, positive resources for erotic justice-making, however, the normative moral tradition must be transformed. That process is currently under way, largely because feminist, womanist, gay/lesbian/bisexual, and Black theological movements are encouraging a methodological shift within Christian ethics. Those on the underside of history are shifting the moral task from an *apologetic* project (what must lesbian and nonlesbian women, gay men, and other nonnormative persons do in order to fit into the tradition?) to a *reconstructive* one (how can Christian tradition be enlarged in order to appropriate new voices and answer the needs of marginalized people for dignity and community?). In light of this methodological challenge, what does a profeminist, antiracist, and sex-positive rereading of Christian tradition offer for the renewal of sexual ethics?

Christianity's Negative Legacy

Christianity is neither a static nor a monolithic tradition when it comes to moral questions. Christian communities in their historical and cultural diversity have addressed various aspects of human life and, in so doing, have communicated differing, even contradictory perspectives on issues ranging from war and peace to poverty, slavery, and capital punishment. Popular notions persist, however, that morality, when all is said and done, is reducible to "private" matters of sexual propriety ("morals"). Moreover, many assume that the church has been singularly preoccupied with sexuality and has maintained a single, unified teaching on this topic down through the ages. These historically inaccurate yet ideologically powerful claims are reinforced whenever the theological tradition is read in a highly selective manner or when earlier faith communities are narrowly interpreted through the lens of contemporary social struggles.

In reading the Christian past, we should stay alert to how our values and loyalties shape our historical perceptions. "To some extent," Beverly Harrison acknowledges, "we all see in the past what we want or need to find there, given our present value commitments."[4] In addition, we ought not assume too quickly that the selected ethical writings from a given period, especially the prescriptions of a few famous theologians, actually represent the morals or the ethical concerns of the majority of Christians at that time. Newer approaches in social and cultural history are recovering great diversity in attitudes and practices among everyday believers and therefore give us reason to question whether, as yet, we know with much accuracy what most Christians of the past, especially women and other marginalized persons, really understood or cared about sexuality and family life.

Although Christian teachings on sexuality are complex and reflect various changes and developments, certain themes about body, sexuality, and a right ordering of sexual relations took hold in the early centuries of the church and continue to be influential. The dominant theological tradition is patriarchal in outlook and negative in tone, so much so that suspicion, avoidance, restriction, and ongoing regulation have been the watchwords about sex, the body, and women's lives in particular. From Augustine to Aquinas, from radical asceticism to the penitentials, characteristic motifs are repeated in Christian responses to sexuality: Sex is an alien and dangerous force that must be contained; sin is loss of control over the body and especially capitulation to sexual desires; women are associated with body, emotionality, and "lower" nature and must therefore be supervised and kept under control for their own good and for men's safety; sex itself is redeemed only by serving a purpose outside itself, namely, procreation; and (male) homosexual activity is condemned because in the sexual act one partner is passive (the female) and the other active (the male), and it is demeaning for a man to behave like a woman (or to be treated as a subordinate). This moral legacy, so very solemn, fearful, and cautious about sex, women, and sexual difference, sees sexuality perennially as a problem. Control is mandated as the necessary Christian moral response to sexuality.[5]

Catholic moral theologian Daniel Maguire speaks of a regrettable turn in the history of the church, beginning with the Constantinian establishment, toward "pelvic theology" and its obsession with sexual control. As the church shifted in the third and fourth centuries from prophetic to establishment status, no longer defining its identity by its resistance to the imperial state and its cult, the hierarchy asserted power by controlling the sexual behavior of believers and creating a heightened clerical image for itself. Citing Samuel Laeuchli's historical investigation of the Council of Elvira (309 C.E.), Maguire observes that the church turned increasingly to sex in order to define both orthodoxy and clerical authority. This "Elvira syndrome" continues to operate today whenever church elites project a narrowly clerical image of the church and rely upon sexual control as a primary tool for that project. As Maguire conjectures, "Contrary to popular myth, Constantine did not convert to Christianity. Christianity converted to Constantine, and Elvira signals the first symptoms of this perversion."[6]

Three assumptions are characteristic of this imperial approach to Christian sexual morals. First, moral truth is located in the past, in a tradition defined by patriarchal authority. A single, definitive position on sexuality is presumed adequate for all times and places. Second, theological discourse about sexuality and moral meanings proceeds in a highly abstract, ahistorical, and largely deductive manner. The conversation has been overwhelmingly one-way in asking " 'What does our *religion* (or the scripture or the tradition or the religious authorities) say about the body and its sexuality?' The assumption [is] that religion [has] its truth, received

61

or arrived at quite independently of our bodily-sexual experience, which then [needs] only to be applied."[7] And third, there is deep suspicion of advocates speaking out of their particular moral struggles, especially those who appear self-interested in making ethical claims. Religious elites have proceeded on an assumption that they are offering a disinterested, "pure" ethic that rises above the rancor of social divisions and is untainted by particular biases or interests.

Assumptions of a Liberating Ethic

A liberating sexual ethic requires shifting to a participatory, communal mode of ethical inquiry. It operates with assumptions quite different from the traditional ethic. First, moral truth is located not only in the past, but is grasped anew as communities and conscientious people in the here and now encounter new circumstances and inquire how the past may offer insight and direction. Moral truth claims are always limited, partial, and related to context. They change as the conditions of human life shift and as people wrestle to formulate their most considered moral judgments amid competing claims and uncertainties.

Second, reappropriation of the past is never a matter of applying past truths to present issues, but is rather a creative, dynamic process of engaging (and being engaged by) a living, pluriform tradition involved in its own continual adaptation and change. A responsible reading of the past requires an awareness of the diversity of voices within the tradition itself, a critical examination of their strengths and weaknesses, and an ongoing dialogue between past and present. This dialogue proceeds as a two-way conversation in which the present questions the past and the past questions the present. Although inherited wisdom from the past is honored, it is granted authority only to the degree, ethicist Larry Rasmussen explains, that "it reveals to us the basic truths of our faith while at the same time honoring the power and authority of our own experience of God alongside that of [earlier] communities," including biblical communities. It is this dialogical method which offers the best hope for doing justice to the notion of a living God and a living faith tradition.[8]

A liberating ethic is aware that the past makes claims on the present. The past in all its diversity has carried the story of God's liberating, redeeming presence and power and has given powerful shape to people's life stories. At the same time, whatever insight may come from the past is dependent upon and filtered through, always through, the interests and limitations of the present community as it recognizes and values its past. The present, therefore, also makes claims on the past. We may engage the past freely and critically, claiming our responsibilities as authoritative interpreters and shapers of the Christian tradition in company with many others, some of whom we will agree with and others we will not.

The dominant tradition has obscured the way justice holds a central place in biblical faith and its ongoing importance for restoring the vitality of contemporary faith communities. Marginal communities have rediscovered that the biblical God is a God of liberation whose passion is for justice shared across all the earth. In an open-ended process of reinterpreting and appropriating the tradition, those of us on the margins today claim our right to evaluate and transform the tradition in light of our experience of God as a God of liberation, not oppression. This liberating God, much to our amazement, delights in our sexuality and our dignity as splendid body-selves in community with other body-selves. In light of this theological vision, our primary accountability is not narrowly to religious tradition or to the past for its own sake, but to present communities of faithful women, gay men, and others who are wrestling with their faith heritage and struggling in church and society for justice and the earth's integrity.

Third, a liberation ethic assumes that no source for ethical insight, past or present, stands alone or is exempt from moral scrutiny in terms of how it impacts the lives of women and marginalized men of all colors. Furthermore, no source is inherently authoritative, but is declared trustworthy by those who discover its value and draw upon its power. As theologian Carter Heyward suggests, "We should always ask this question: Does [this resource] help us realize more fundamentally our connectedness to one another and hence the shape of our identities as persons-in-relation?"[9] An authority becomes valuable if it calls forth our desire for justice for all peoples, including ourselves.

This relational, dialogical approach to moral authority gives primary weight to the present, but more explicitly to those committed to and actively engaged in pursuing justice. As African American feminist theorist bell hooks puts the matter, "It is important that we speak. *What* we speak about is more important."[10] What is worth speaking about, and advocating passionately for, from a liberation perspective is whatever allows people on the margins to live, assert their dignity, lay claim to their fair share, and persist against the odds.

Re-centering the Moral Conversation

Redressing the inadequacies of inherited Christian morals about human sexuality requires much more than minor adjustments at the tradition's edges or tinkering with this or that specific concern. The dominant ethical paradigm is deeply flawed. The Christian tradition is fearful of sex, yet fixated on its power. Racist patriarchal Christianity holds on to a legalistic, largely punitive moral code; it supports misogyny, racism, and homophobia; and it fails to provide a workable ethical framework for a justice-seeking faith community. We are encumbered, are we not, by a legacy that encourages a distorted, largely reactive view of the erotic dimensions of our lives? The dominant Christian tradition leads people to believe that sexuality is a dangerous, alien force having greater significance than other aspects of human life. This will no longer do.

How people think about, engage in, and evaluate moral advocacy in regard to sexuality must be assessed holistically and systemically rather than in a fragmentary, piecemeal fashion. The very categories and interpretive lenses used for reflection must be chosen with care. How we think about these matters has consequences for persons and communities. As Larry Rasmussen proposes, "the categories we think *with* as we think *about* something are vital for the moral content and outcome." In addition, we need to register how " 'the worst, the most corrupting lies are problems poorly [or wrongly] stated'."[11] Our inherited moral tradition consistently defines the sexual problem wrongly. It fears sexual difference and diversity. It renders the victims of sexual violence and oppression invisible. It diverts energy away from sexual justice. It privatizes our pain.

A serious moral realignment about sexuality is in order. Theological thinking must be brought into line, first of all, with the best scientific knowledge available. During the last thirty-five years, more information has been accumulated than ever before about the complex biological/ psychological/social/spiritual process of human sexual development, about the various patterns of human sexual response and behavior, and about the varieties of marriage, family, and partnership systems. Sex researchers and therapists are quick to point out, however, that "almost all of our new knowledge is in conflict with traditional religious belief systems." Thus, as William Stayton, an American Baptist minister and sex therapist, concludes, "our religious institutions [must be] challenged to their core in order to be helpful and relevant to the sexual concerns of our time."[12] At the same time, scientific perspectives must also be assessed in terms of whether they reflect or dislodge sexist, racist, and heterosexist values. Social and natural sciences often replicate the prevailing control paradigm, reinforce cultural patterns of male dominance and female subjugation, and provide further legitimation of compulsory heterosexuality in secular guise.[13]

While scientific wisdom may help us appreciate the complex contours of human sexual experience, the primary impetus for reappraising Christian sexual ethics comes from a different source. Conventional Christian sexual morals must be criticized because of the churches' moral myopia and complicity in sexual oppression. Women and gay/lesbian/bisexual persons of all colors are consistently devalued by this tradition. Domestic and sexual violence have been ignored as serious moral concerns. Few persons find adequate resources from their churches about how to live gracefully in their bodies or how to integrate sexuality and spirituality. Few religious people exhibit confidence and joy as sexual persons.

Because gay men, lesbian women, and bisexual persons of all colors are placed by Christian moral convention outside the boundaries of moral respectability, and because we are also regularly castigated as "unrepentant sinners" by virtue of our sexuality, we must ask: Should we turn at all to such a tradition for guidance?[14] Many people respond in the negative because conventional Christian morality places their self-respect in jeopardy. Many gay people, as well as women of faith, express this reservation. Because of the churches' complicity in women's oppression and "the long centuries of failure of vision that [have] allowed sexism to flourish *in spite of the best moral insights of their traditions*," many women are wary about any religious teaching about sexuality and their lives.[15] For many, considerable effort is required to keep open the question whether the faith tradition can offer reliable guidance with respect to human sexuality.

Others, like me, are painfully aware of the difficulties involved in releasing the patriarchal hold on Western religious consciousness. At the same time, while contending with Christian tradition, we embrace this faith heritage as our own. We refuse to jettison the past or hand it over to patriarchal authorities to claim for themselves. Rather, our wager is that the sex-negativity within Catholic and Protestant traditions is largely a distortion of their own central values and that sexual healing and transformation are possible. Our task is to reclaim what is most authentic and life-affirming from these faith traditions.

In this work of reclamation we are not looking for, nor are we expecting to find, some nonpatriarchal, noncorrupted essence of a Christian past that can be applied to the present. Rather, we intentionally locate ourselves as struggling *inside* and *with* the tradition. Our hope is that we may disarm its oppressiveness, reshape it in positive directions, and secure a liberating spiritual home that welcomes our sexualities and therefore welcomes us.

This wager is not made lightly. It has been forged out of hard-won knowledge that the Christian tradition has been a source of danger and pain, but something more as well. For many people of color, some women, some gay men, and other marginalized persons, Christian faith also is a source of strength and resiliency, a site for moral vision and power, a place for claiming our dignity as sensuous body-selves, and a haven for sustaining our commitment to live toward communal right relation across race, gender, and class differences. Some of us stay in—or come back to—church despite its rigidity, dysfunction, and resistance to change because we seek a faith community that honors us and our God-experience and encourages us to persist on our respective faith journeys. In the midst of church or from outside, persons marginalized by sexual injustice are the ones who must protest and call for moral transformation. Harmed by present arrangements, we have little reason to make excuses for the moral wrongness of received tradition.

Until recently, elite church leaders have set the terms of the conversation about sexuality and spirituality. Marginalized people have contributed little to shaping the Christian moral tradition because they have lacked sufficient visibility, standing, or resources to define the normative faith community on their terms. Questions about who constitutes church, whose voices are taken seriously, and whose perspectives carry authoritative weight are now being asked. Those on the margins are claiming a place in the midst of the theological conversation and asserting their power to reshape the tradition. This is a "new thing," causing the very foundations of the church and its patriarchal traditions to shake.

To be adequate, a liberating Christian ethic must address power issues forthrightly, be committed to the participation of the full community, actively welcome those on the margin of church and society, and be prepared for a new thing. What Judith Plaskow says of feminists within Judaism also applies to feminists within Christianity: "As Jewish women recognize ourselves as heirs to and shapers of Judaism, as we explore our own experiences and integrate them into the tradition, we necessarily transform the tradition and shape it into something new." Furthermore, "If we are Jews not despite being feminists but *as feminists*, then Judaism will have to change—we will have to work to change it—to make a whole identity possible."[16]

The larger moral project here is not simply to add on women of all colors, gay men, and others onto an otherwise unaltered tradition. The intent of liberating ethics is to transform the tradition itself, so that it is no longer a male, heterosexual tradition but an inclusive, hospitable tradition sufficiently enlarged to welcome those it previously disempowered. As women, gay men, and others enter more fully into the theological conversation, we bear witness to the fact that the more inclusive any community is of persons, perspectives, and life experiences, the better chance it has of rendering a truthful account of our common humanity including our sexualities.

The intent of liberating moral praxis has moved well beyond inclusion or equal access within the present order. The more substantive work is to change the rules of church and society that rank difference in terms of superiority and subordination. We insist that all persons, ourselves included, are entitled to the basic resources needed for a life worth living, but also that we all have the right to shape moral discourse and articulate for ourselves what gives meaning and purpose to our lives. Furthermore, all persons have a fundamental moral right to love and be loved—sexually, as well as spiritually. We also have a moral right for our love to inform and deepen our understandings of God, the human condition, community, salvation, and all other faith claims.

Sustained engagement in the struggle for sexual justice has given us some glimmer of hope for transforming community toward greater respect and care for human difference, but there are no guarantees. With no guarantees of success, justice-seeking Christians must be energized— and directed—not so much by the past ("What in the tradition is ours? What can we claim that has not also wounded us?"[17]), but rather by what theologian Peggy Way calls an "authority of possibility,"[18] a vision of a transformed religious heritage that offers genuine strength because it has been recast intentionally as profeminist, antiracist, and gay-positive. People of faith marginalized by sexual oppression yearn with a deep spiritual hunger for a Christianity genuinely respectful of our dignity as persons and responsive to our needs for justice and love.

The fundamental ground rule for liberating sexual ethics is that voices from the margin must be brought into the center of the conversation *on their own terms*. Those with social privilege earn the right to speak and to question by first listening to and taking seriously those voices long discounted and silenced. Because of white-skin privilege and other advantages of gender, class, and marital status, the responsible exercise of our theological power requires first that we use whatever relative power we possess to encourage the disenfranchised to speak and share their faith, struggles, and hope. That sharing should proceed only on terms that enhance the power of the disenfranchised. Second, we must open ourselves up for questioning, challenge, and renewal by those not like us. Justice-making, therefore, is not a *doing for* those "less fortunate" by those better positioned, but rather an ongoing commitment to *live respectfully with and for* each other and to be held mutually accountable for the character of our communal ties. The shape of our communities, the presence or absence of genuine diversity, our commitment to enter into mutual accountability, and our willingness to be changed all greatly affect the character and content of our moral discourse.

From Apology
to Reconstruction

A justice-focused theological ethic cannot rest satisfied with an apologetic stance toward Christian tradition. It cannot be concerned with making excuses for a sex-negative Christianity or with asking marginalized people to "fit in with" a settled, unalterable tradition that claims for itself an authority exempt from criticism and moral accountability. Rather, a liberating ethic honors the humanity of those oppressed by sexual injustice and seeks to re-create a Christianity that can welcome their presence and advocate their rights for dignity and a full life.

The reconstruction of the faith tradition moves forward on the basis of two assumptions. First, the sources for Christian theological reflection, including scripture, church teaching, insight from other disciplines, and contemporary experience, should be regarded as valuable resources with only relative authority but not as final arbiters or controls. All resources must be evaluated in light of the needs of marginalized communities in their movement toward justice.

New Testament scholar Elisabeth Schüssler Fiorenza recommends approaching scripture guided by the metaphor of "bread not stone." She invites feminists to transform "our metaphor of Scripture as 'tablets of stone' on which the unchanging word of God is engraved for all times into the image of bread that nurtures, sustains, and energizes women as people of God in our struggles against injustice and oppression."[19] Ethicist Gary Comstock speaks similarly of the benefits for gay, lesbian, and bisexual people in thinking of Christian sources, including the Bible, as "friend" rather than "parent." Instead of seeking approval from the Bible as a (negative) parental authority, gay people should acknowledge the limits and errors of biblical traditions, especially about homosexuality. After all, Comstock notes, much that is also said in the Bible about women, slavery, and dietary laws is no longer accepted today as authoritative, nor should it be. We are free to grant new authority to this resource, he continues, by engaging it "as I would a friend—as one to whom I have made a commitment and in whom I have invested dearly, but with whom I insist on a mutual exchange of critique, encouragement, support, and challenge." This stance empowers gay, lesbian, bisexual people and their supporters to confront as well as "receive" the Bible. "As with my friends," Comstock explains, "I criticize and call it to account for its homophobia."[20] A liberating ethic calls for critique and reconstruction of the past, not apologies for its negative impact on persons and communities.

A second assumption of a liberating sexual ethic is that Christian tradition is far more diverse and expansive than represented by patriarchal voices and the dominant sex-negative, racist, misogynistic, and homophobic legacy of Christian moral teaching. What Walter Brueggemann says about the Bible applies more generally to the pluriform Christian tradition: "The popular mind . . . regards the Bible as a seamless cloth with a unified teaching." The truth of the matter, however, is that "the Bible present[s] powerful theological views in deep tension with each other, if not in contradiction to each other. Responsible use of the Bible requires the effort to notice the differences and to sort them out."[21] Scripture and tradition are pluralistic. The question is not whether to accept or reject the past as such, but rather how to identify the proper criteria for sorting out what continues to be revelatory and may therefore bear good news for us. What is our principle of selection? How do we discern theologically what is authoritative from what is not?

A profeminist, antiracist, and gay-positive ethic answers these questions only by staying grounded in, and accountable to, the liberation praxis of what ethicist Daniel Spencer calls the "community at the margins."[22] This community intentionally resists sexism, racism, and heterosexism and celebrates the moral agency of women, gay men, and all others seeking justice. Justice-committed Christians understand marginality as a gift and as a burden. Marginality offers a space of radical openness, a place in which to see things differently, imagine alternatives, and gain fresh perspective. In this sense, marginality is something one may cling to, bell hooks contends, "because it nourishes one's capacity to resist."[23] From this site of freedom, gay/lesbian/bisexual people, survivors of sexual violence, and many others can gain critical distance, claim their authority as moral agents, speak their voices as theological subjects, and find stamina with which to engage the broader community.

The moral task for justice advocates is never simply to preserve and transmit canonical texts or traditions. Rather we must evaluate and reappropriate all traditions in a discerning manner. A justice hermeneutic or interpretive lens allows us to proceed in a critical, self-reflective manner about human sexuality and Christian faith. We work with the presumption, tested by our own experiences of struggle and survival, that what is genuinely of God embraces the goodness of our sexualities, enhances our dignity as persons, strengthens us for community, and deepens our capacity to resist evil and celebrate life. Faithfulness also requires of us a passionate searching for right-relatedness with God, self, others, and the earth. A liberative Christian ethic operates, therefore, with some specific interpretive guidelines. Whatever in scripture, tradition, reason, and experience embodies genuine love and caring justice, *as defined by a radically diverse, justice-focused faith community at the margins*, is what bears authority for our lives. Whatever in biblical tradition, church practice and teaching, human experience and reason violates the command to do justice, love kindness, and walk humbly with God (Micah 6:8), *as defined by a radically diverse, justice-focused church at the margins*, is what must be denied ethical authority. A Christian ethic that lacks a central, unshakable commitment to sexual justice and communal well-being is not worth anyone's bother, except to criticize as a poor substitute for the real thing.

Rereading the Tradition with New Eyes

Reading scripture and tradition is a political activity that either supports or challenges unjust power structures. To a great extent, the politics of *sustaining, not resisting* oppression determine how most white, middle-class Protestants read and appropriate the past. Progressive, justice-focused Christians approach scripture and tradition out of an entirely different political and moral sensibility, namely, to expose Christian complicity in injustice of all kinds and to make imaginable a profeminist, antiracist, sex-positive Christianity.

Placing subjugated peoples, including racial/ethnic and poor women and men, at the hermeneutical center of moral discourse is not an exclusionary measure. Such recentering is an intentional political-oppositional strategy to challenge injustice. Introjecting the voices and moral wisdom of the disenfranchised majority from the margins engages them *as subjects and shapers* of the theological conversation instead of distancing them as silenced objects.

A justice hermeneutic is not interested in flipping the sex/gender hierarchy upside down, or condemning white males, or devaluing married heterosexual people. Privileged people often fear that radical social change means nothing more than a reversal of social positions, such that today's oppressed become tomorrow's oppressors. Because they lack a genuinely transcendent moral vision, those occupying power positions in the current pecking order have cause to fear that when justice is served they might well be placed on the receiving end of the injustices they have handed out so unmercifully to others. That ominous specter, that the structures of injustice are frozen and unalterable, means that only the personnel—the players—may change, but not the structures—the playing field—that perpetuate alienation and exploitation. Because of the tenacity of the dominant paradigm and its hold on people's imaginations, moving away from a paradigm that assumes the normativity of dominant-subordinate relations is a daunting task. What elicits genuine moral passion for radical, at-the-roots transformation is not people's suffering or their fears, but rather their capacity to imagine an alternative possibility. The vision that compels is that of a renewed, revitalized social order in which people can relate as social equals and together build a beloved community. A justice ethic invites all people to exercise their moral imaginations and accept accountability for how their actions affect others and the earth itself. Placing those most affected by injustice at the center of moral discourse is a deliberate strategy to break with the dominant paradigm.

Marginalized people bring to theological ethics a healthy skepticism about institutionalized Christianity and how scripture and tradition have been used to oppress people. Although biblical texts are sometimes misinterpreted and quoted out of context (prooftexting), the larger problem is that the Bible itself is a patriarchal document. Its texts communicate patriarchal values and render women, gay people, and others either invisible or as the subjugated Other. A liberating ethic must adopt a twofold approach to the Christian past. On the one hand, a hermeneutics of *suspicion* is needed which, as Schüssler Fiorenza says, "takes as its starting point the assumption that biblical texts and their interpretations are androcentric and serve patriarchal functions." On the other hand, a hermeneutics of *remembrance* is needed to recover stories of resistance to injustice and to honor the biblical heritage not simply as a history of oppression, but also as a history of liberation and struggle. Disenfranchised women and men have been empowered by the Spirit to protest and work for a new moral order.[24]

Two examples, one from the Hebrew scriptures and the other from the gospel traditions, illustrate the possibility of reclaiming biblical sources for a liberating sexual ethic. The first is the Song of Songs. This love poem offers a startling vision of sexual friendship and passionate loving between a man and a woman. Their relationship is nonhierarchical and nonexploitative. Feminist biblical scholar Phyllis Trible argues that this poem celebrates sexuality without shame or fear. "Eroticism," she notes, "becomes worship in the context of grace." In addition, sexual intimacy takes place without male domination, female subordination, or gender stereotyping. "Throughout the Song [the woman] is independent, fully the equal of the man. Although at times he approaches her, more often she initiates their meetings." Finally, the Song of Songs' imaging of sexuality departs from the traditional patriarchal emphases on procreation and control of women's bodies. "Never is this woman called a wife, nor is she required to bear children." In fact, no mention is made of marriage or the duty to restrict sex to the marriage context. As Trible concludes, "Love for the sake of love is its message."[25]

For constructing a liberating sexual ethic, the Song of Songs offers strong biblical affirmation of the goodness of the body, erotic passion, and the gift of pleasure. Its sex-positive voice is refreshing within a religious heritage that has been largely fearful of sexuality. Gay theologian Gary Comstock argues that the Song of Songs is "*the* only part of the Bible with which we can form an alliance for constructing a sexual ethics based on the interests and needs of people for body pleasure." Even that judgment must be qualified, Comstock reasons, on two scores. First, "this Song is but a few pages among a thousand, and it tends to be one of the most ignored books of the Bible." Second, the portrayal of sexuality in this text is thoroughly heterosexual. It gives gay men and lesbian women no acknowledgment or affirmation of their dignity and moral integrity.[26]

Comstock is right that the couple portrayed in the Song is unabashedly heterosexual. When viewed by itself, their heterosexuality may indeed reinforce the normative exclusivity of heterosexual coupling in Hebraic and later Christian traditions. It may be a mistake, however, to emphasize the couple's heterosexuality to the point of overshadowing a more subversive aspect of this biblical narrative. Although the couple portrayed in the Song is clearly heterosexual, that fact may be less significant than their challenge to, and disregard of, prevailing cultural expectations about what constitutes normative loving. When this narrative is read critically through a justice lens, the Song of Songs appears to be not so much a "simple" love poem, but more a polemical protest song. This protest poem celebrates and even flaunts the moral beauty of a couple's love because they stand *in violation of* prevailing cultural norms.

Womanist biblical scholar Renita J. Weems has carefully uncovered a hidden polemic within the Song. As an African-American woman, Weems has paid attention to the color imagery of this text and noticed how the female lover is portrayed as a dark-skinned, small-breasted woman. Her physical beauty is at odds with the prevailing cultural standards of her time. Therefore the Song is interested in highlighting more than the goodness of physicality and sexual pleasure, or even this woman's boldness in expressing her sexual desire for her lover. As Weems explains, "some aspect(s) of the lovers' relationship were in contradiction to prevailing norm." Moreover, the text's narrator "attempts to uncover and debunk the respectable prejudices of her audience in her defense of their right to love one another." This counter-cultural critic moves, therefore, beyond naming the passionate love of two heterosexual partners as beautiful and right. In a more pointed fashion, the poet names as beautiful and right the love of two *nonnormative* lovers. As Weems contends, "They are two lovers whom society, for inscrutable reasons, sought to keep apart, perhaps because they were from different classes, from different ethnic backgrounds, or of a different color."[27] This Song criticizes the dominant social order because of its sexual injustice. Sexual injustice is a tell-tale sign of moral dis-order more broadly construed.

This biblical text challenges the community to rethink its categorization of normative, as well as transgressive, sexuality. The community is not to limit love's embrace to "normative bodies" alone, but rather is called upon to welcome mutual love between any and all lovers committed to each other's well-being and mutual delight. More than a love poem, the Song of Songs offers a powerful critique of culture and of the religious establishment's sexual oppressiveness. As Weems notes, "It adjures us . . . not to impose on relationships our own biased preconceptions about what is appropriate and inappropriate sexual behavior, who makes a suitable mate and who does not."[28]

Here scripture, when read through a justice hermeneutic, offers a critique of tradition and "new eyes" to affirm on biblical grounds the beauty and moral integrity of love in unexpected places, including between interracial couples, people with disabilities, and same-sex couples. A justice hermeneutic calls into question interpretations that privatize, and depoliticize, sexual love by abstracting it from political, cultural, and religious struggles. The sexuality portrayed in this biblical text has been shaped by social injustice. The Song protests against the dominant religious community's complicity in that injustice. A hermeneutics of suspicion is necessary to discern the racist, sexist, and heterosexist character of sexual injustice. Otherwise we may not be in a position to "hear more" from this text or be confronted by the Song's political significance.

A contemporary Christian sexual ethic also requires critical reflection on the gospel traditions by those on the margins who discern a new leading of the Spirit. Reading scripture in a discerning manner requires asking what is compatible and what is not compatible with the vision and values of the Jesus story as this story informs and is enriched by the stories of communities struggling for survival and a decent future. A central biblical affirmation is that the moral life is an expression of gratitude to God's loving presence. As God is gracious, merciful, and compassionate, so we are called forth to be and do likewise: to be gracious, merciful, and compassionate people.[29] Another conviction is that God's power for new life, dramatically revealed in Jesus' life and ministry, makes life new by reordering relationships between and among people. The baptismal liturgy Paul quotes in Galatians 3:28, "There is neither Jew nor Greek, there is neither slave nor free, there is neither male nor female; for you are all one in Christ Jesus," reflects this commitment and transformative possibility throughout early Christianity.

In response to the destabilizing, antihierarchical movement of the Spirit, early Christian communities were impelled to eliminate social and religious barriers between persons, to set aside purity regulations in favor of corporate justice, and to move toward greater inclusivity and equality. On none of these fronts, however,—the elimination of ethnic and religious barriers, the relative devaluation of purity concerns, or the restructuring of social relations—was there anything approaching unanimity among early Christians. Different voices within the New Testament faith communities drew differing conclusions about how to relate the gospel to particular situations. Some, like Paul, insisted that the gospel demanded egalitarian relations between men and women. Others, like the authors of Ephesians, Colossians, and the Pastoral Epistles, argued that the gospel demanded the shoring up of patriarchal arrangements.

Throughout the New Testament we find evidence of a struggle, at once political and spiritual, between those who adapted the egalitarian Jesus tradition to fit, once again, within a hierarchical status quo, and those who resisted such accommodation. The diversity and moral conflicts within the New Testament communities are similar to the theological diversity and moral conflicts within contemporary faith communities. Each generation and every faith community must discern the gospel and its ethical demands while remaining open to God's continuing movement. Justice-seeking Christians affirm that the God of Jesus is not a god of oppression, but rather the Spirit of liberation and of a new life lived abundantly in right relation with the earth and all peoples.

From a justice perspective, the normative character of pluriform New Testament witnesses is located, on the one hand, in the ongoing process of contextualized theological discernment and, on the other hand, in the particular moral path that disciples of Jesus should follow. Living faithfully in community requires freedom and equality with all other persons. Moreover, mutual love, justice as right-relatedness, and restraint of personal liberty by the powerful for the well-being of the less powerful take precedence over social convention and concern for respectability. New life in Christ creates heightened expectations of social relations that are no longer bound by established social structures, purity regulations, or ethnic and religious barriers. Early Christians in many respects drew socially disruptive conclusions from the gospel. They concluded that religious and ethnic barriers were no longer germane. They dispensed with circumcision as a requirement for membership, freed slaves, and were bold enough to alter sabbath practice. They concluded that matters of ritual purity, particularly regarding table fellowship, were no longer relevant. Some also concluded that the patriarchal household belonged to an old order that was passing away and therefore no longer held authority for them.

Concerning each of these matters, early Christians claimed a radical freedom in Christ. At the same time, they did not complete the task of interpretation and application of the gospel, nor did they imagine that they could do so. That task continues. While early Christians set a direction in moving toward a normative vision of communal holiness as inclusive wholeness,[30] they did not always consistently follow their own direction or moral impulse. Some Christians refused to grant women equal status in church and family. Others found no tension between owning slaves and being Christian. Still others held onto the prohibition against homosexuality even though this restriction reflected the kind of purity concern that many early Christian communities set aside in other respects, including the Jew/gentile, clean/unclean distinction.

Today, as in the past, battles over inclusivity and ending gender, race, and sexual injustice continue within religious communities. For liberation Christians, the human vocation is to re-make community so that all persons may experience the vitality and integrity of their lives, as well as contribute to each other's mutual well-being. The sacred movement of the Spirit is revealed in our full-bodied yearning for mutual relation and communal well-being. A powerful reclaiming of this sacred Spirit takes place whenever people assert their power to seek communal justice, to name the Sacred for themselves, and to draw their own conclusions about the gospel for their times.

In joining this movement, we may recognize ourselves as heirs to a freedom tradition, no matter how marginal or fragile that tradition appears to be. We are recipients of an awesome, though long ignored, moral legacy from those who preceded us in the faith and refused to reconcile either God or themselves to oppression. When we hunger and thirst for justice, they become our people, and we become theirs. Their God is our God, and our passion for justice only increases.

A liberating Christian sexual ethic resonates deeply with this passionate call for a new order of righteousness. In order to craft such an ethic, we must make a clear, definitive, and unapologetic break with the Christian tradition's sex-negativity, oppression of women and gay people, and rigidity about right loving and good sex. Breaking with patriarchal Christianity, however, is not enough. We must also embrace the more marginal, justice-oriented sub-traditions as our own wisdom tradition.

Both the Song of Songs and the Jesus tradition, when read through the experiential lenses of marginalized persons in resistance to sexual injustice, encourage us to upend the status quo and insist on a radical rearticulation of the normative religious tradition. In chapter 4 I explore more explicitly a reconstruction of Christian sexual ethics that reflects a biblical "vision of possibility" and delights in a body-affirming, justice-centered sensuality.

4

Reimagining Good Sex
The Eroticizing of Mutual Respect and Pleasure

> For matters moral, I suggest we engage in
> creative listening, sketch some general directions, and
> leave the rest up to the good sense of faithful people.[1]
>
> —Mary Hunt

The moral problematic about sexuality in this culture is that racist patriarchy annexes body pleasure and attaches it to injustice. Many people find themselves erotically aroused only by dominant/subordinate power relations. They accept these patterns as normative and entirely natural. Progressive people, therefore, in religious communities and elsewhere, have their work cut out for them if they intend to confront this humanly corrupting state of affairs. Eroticizing equality and mutual respect as the normative expectation for all social interaction lies at the heart of challenging every social oppression.

Reversing the workings of a patriarchal culture that eroticizes gender, race, and other injustices will not come easily. Both personal and sociocultural transformations are needed. As Beverly Harrison observes, "the tragedy of our so-called sexual morality is that mutual respect and eroticism are utterly separated in the lives of most people." As if that were not enough, people who "lack a genuine power of eroticism . . . assuage their emptiness by controlling others."[2] As I discussed in chapter 2, the eroticization of male gender supremacy allows many men to believe that coercing an intimate partner, whether male or female, feels good. Women are encouraged to believe that being overpowered by a partner is pleasurable or at least tolerable. White supremacy, ableism, and other social dynamics work in conjunction with misogyny to reinforce the cultural link between eroticism and injustice. The powerful presume they are entitled to control others. They feel their entitlement deep in their bones. The less powerful feel obligated to be securely placed under someone else's control. They feel fear and guilt if they venture to cross the line. Inequities of power and status are naturalized as something that feels right to people, close to their skins.

If we fail to see how patriarchal eroticism has electrified injustice and made it titillating, we will not grasp why so many people manage to rest comfortably with oppression, their own and that of others. Why is it that people not only tolerate injustice, but do so with smiles on their faces? Could it be that injustice corrupts at the body level and, therefore, at the core of our personhood? Could injustice not dissipate the human longing for real companionship across a multitude of social differences or numb our social affections altogether? Whenever oppression rubs day and night against the body, people end up not only thinking about but also *somatizing* racism, sexism, heterosexism, and cultural elitism. These power distortions are felt in, through, and by their bodies. All this affects how they carry their bodies, move their arms and legs, hold their heads, and occupy space in relation to others. People internalize in their bodies, not simply in their psyches, the belief that injustice feels good and safe. Considerable effort will therefore be needed to unlearn our embodied social alienation and, conversely, to appropriate a desire, at a sufficiently deep level, for social relations that are respectful of all people.

The renewal of Christian sexual ethics, in any meaningful sense, requires taking on an extensive project of moral transformation. On the one hand, we must invite people into a process of unlearning the culturally inculcated eroticized desire for power as control. On the other hand, we must teach the value of mutual vulnerability and interdependency in all our connections. Moral education must specifically address what it means to take responsibility for doing what is right and pleasurable with our bodies. For some people, physical touch, including genital touching, will take place primarily or exclusively within a committed relationship. When all goes well, sex enhances an intimacy already established. For others, sex will be an initial avenue for exploring bodily connection with another and for opening up the possibility of further intimacy and friendship.

Accepting sexual touch as a moral resource flies in the face of racist, patriarchal norms. However, mutual pleasuring undertaken with tenderness and respect is a crucial, though widely neglected, component of Christian moral formation. Conventional sexual ethics have not only discouraged such exploration, but have weighed it down with the sternest approbation. The denial of pleasure is characteristic of oppressive systems. Any social order—or religious ethic, for that matter—that discourages people from trusting their feelings, especially their sensuality, or from enjoying their bodies will be experienced as oppressive to the human spirit. Instead of trying to restrain sexual expression through fear, shame, and other social sanctions, we should be enhancing people's interest in and growth toward mature intimacy relations. We need an ethic that appreciates how we become sexually mature persons only through an extended process of exploration and not magically by going through any single life passage (e.g., entering into marriage). We need, but do not yet have, an ethic that would equip us both to enjoy our freedom and to assume our responsibility as sexual beings. We must learn to honor ourselves as lifelong students of erotic discovery, self-awareness, and delight.

The renewal of Christian sexual ethics also requires greater candor about the widening gap between official church teaching about sex and the actual lives of most people. This gap has developed—not as conservatives argue—because people are suddenly less conscientious, but because the conventional religious moral code ("celibacy in singleness, sex only in marriage") is woefully outdated and inadequate. Dissatisfaction with conventional sexual morality is increasing, and for good reason, among young and old, male and female, gay and nongay, married and single persons. No sexual ethic, Christian or otherwise, can claim moral credibility if it is constructed upon human suffering and body alienation.

Our task is nothing less than to break the eroticized link between pleasure and injustice. Rampant fear of erotic power undergirds sexualized oppression against women and against gay, lesbian, and bisexual people of all colors. At the same time, all persons, with or without social power, are diminished because of the cultural disparagement of the body and the refusal to accept mutual pleasure as the norm for all intimate relations.[3] Racist patriarchy promotes eroticized fear as a social control mechanism. People learn to distrust the erotic and identify their sexualities, rather than injustice, as the source of their personal pain and sorrow. A liberating ethic must challenge such confusion and make a decisive break with this sex-negativity, but what sort of ethic would make this break possible? What would it mean to honor the erotic as the spark within and between us that values mutuality? This chapter explores the possibility of an ethical eroticism.

Reimagining Erotic Power

In contrast to racist patriarchal views that sex is an alien, destructive force that requires heavy restraints, a liberating Christian ethic welcomes sexual energy as an intrinsic, constitutive component of our humanness. Sexuality is our embodied sensuality and capacity for connection. Sexuality is, therefore, more than an isolated segment of our lives. It extends far beyond genital sexual expression. Persons *are* body-selves. We connect with the world through our senses and through touch. Our sensuality and embodiment as males and females ground our being in the world.

If it is misleading to say that we merely *have* a body, it is also misleading to suggest that sexuality concerns only one's "private" feelings apart from others and the world. Rather, sexuality is our relational capacity to move beyond ourselves toward others. Living passionately in our bodies, living from the center outward (rather than from external scripts), opens us to vital and at times playful interaction with others. Sexuality is a mode of communication, the giving and receiving of recognition and regard. The erotic desire for knowledge—to know and be known by another—goes far beyond the need of the intellect or the genitals. The whole self becomes engaged. We long for an embodied response from another who confirms our individuality, knows us subject-to-subject, and responds to us as a person fully alive. Sexuality infuses personal and social life with energy for connection and mutual recognition.

Theologian Rebecca Parker, in an essay entitled "Making Love as a Means of Grace," writes that sexuality generates joy in being alive. It also reassures us of our personal power to affect others and, in turn, be affected by them. Most importantly, sexuality releases creative energy, a generative power from within that brings forth a distinctive passion or liveliness. Parker explains, "In this way, again, carnal knowledge saves us rather than damns us." By granting us a sense of ourselves as powerful and present to one another, our sexuality draws us to focus on the joy of creating. Through our embodied capacity for sensuality and pleasure, "the zest for passionate, exuberant, creative living can be tasted and seen and thus restored and sustained."[4]

As sensuous human beings, we know and value the world and therefore become self-directing moral agents only as we feel connected in and through our bodies. As Beverly Harrison contends, "*all* our relations to others—to God, to neighbor, to cosmos—[are] mediated through our bodies, which are the locus of our perception and knowledge of the world."[5] Patriarchal Christianity fears deep feeling and therefore negates sexuality, but in doing so it also diminishes moral perception and attentiveness in people. "If feeling is damaged or cut off," Harrison explains, "our power to image the world and act into it is destroyed and our rationality is impaired."[6] Moral knowing is rooted in feeling, and we depend upon sensuality to grasp and value the world. When sexuality is feared and evaded, people lack responsiveness and run the risk of becoming out of touch with what causes joy, suffering, and vulnerability, including their own. A people alienated from their bodies are more likely to be content with, and even at home with, pain and oppression.

A liberating ethic affirms, as Valverde suggests, that "where there is strong eroticism, there is power," including the power to claim one's agency as both lover and beloved.[7] Erotic energy is present in all social interaction, but contrary to patriarchal ideology, erotic desire in and of itself is not dangerous. The danger lies in the misuse of this power against another. In a culture in which inequalities of race, gender, and class are eroticized, one person's power becomes the cause of another person's pain and humiliation. Therein lies the real danger.

Eroticizing equality within every social relation would require an equitable redistribution of power and social goods. It would also encourage people to explore friendship and intimacy with appropriate measures of freedom, playfulness, and respect. When two persons are present to each other and recognize each other as fully human, when each can assume the role of the "knower" and the "known," erotic power sharing can generate deep pleasure between them. This kind of lovemaking can fuel a desire to extend right relation throughout other aspects of their lives. Persons thus experience themselves as desirable and lovable, able to combine action and receptivity, feeling and doing. Their body-mediated erotic power is morally good. As Parker notes, when women and, I dare say, men are erotically empowered, we "feel the force of our soul, the reality of our powerful presence in the world, and we feel it with joy."[8]

Erotic joy is typically disparaged as a moral resource. Frequently, "ethics" is taken to mean strict rules without exception that keep people from doing whatever it is they really want to do. People learn that if an activity feels good to them, they probably should not be doing it, at least not without guilt. The forbidden activity varies, but it may be sex, eating desserts, or taking a day off from work. The ethical here is equated with the negative ("Don't do it!") and with duty, acting *against* one's desires. Pleasure and duty are seen as opposites. Moral minimalism fits neatly with patriarchal antieroticism. It also reinforces the abiding sense of personal inadequacy that plagues so many people in capitalist cultures. People do not trust themselves or their feelings. Patriarchal ethics foster self-hatred.

In contrast, feminist and gay/lesbian/bisexual liberation perspectives are appreciative of materiality, sensuality, and pleasure as ethical guides.[9] If creation, including our humanity, is genuinely good and a source of delight, should we not expect correspondences between what is good and what feels good to us? Would it not be wrong to discount the connection between right conduct and our sense of personal satisfaction, even happiness? A liberation ethic rejects the assumption that delight and pleasure are morally frivolous and fraught with danger.[10] To the contrary, our capacity to take delight in life is an important standard for judging what is worthwhile and useful for ethical living.

Satisfaction should infuse all life activities, not only the explicitly sexual. Audre Lorde, in her essay "Uses of the Erotic: The Erotic as Power," speaks of the erotic as the "nurturer or nursemaid of all our deepest knowledge." When we feel deeply about our life pursuits and the quality of our relationships, we begin to ask that all activities resonate, she writes, "in accordance with that joy which we know ourselves to be capable of." The erotic becomes a source of moral insight, "projected from within each of us, not to settle for the convenient, the shoddy, the conventionally expected, nor the merely safe." Erotic power is our means to say "yes" to life. It insists that actions fit the value of "what is deepest and strongest and richest within each of us."[11]

A feminist and gay liberation ethic challenges the view that eroticism is something merely self-indulgent or a distraction from moral development. Taking the erotic seriously makes us responsible in a new way for using this gift wisely. Centered, self-respecting persons become both responsible to themselves and open to the value of others. Living tenderly into and within our sensuality, we are less likely to become numb to oppression or to ignore our pain or the pain of others. By staying attuned to what feels right to us and by nurturing this awareness in the whole of our lives, we become less willing to tolerate abuse, injustice, and human cruelty. We become more and more desirous of living freely. We therefore also run the risk of becoming a danger to the status quo because of our unwillingness to tolerate abuse and oppression.

Patriarchal Christianity has it wrong: The erotic is not a hostile, alien force lurking from within to bring us to ruin, but is rather an internal moral guidance system, grounded in our body's responsiveness to respectful, loving touch. We have the capacity to comprehend the power of the erotic in our lives and make good choices about its use. We can work through the implications of our feelings, sexual and otherwise. In doing so, we gain confidence in ourselves as thinking, feeling, acting subjects who can respond to life's demands as our own persons, from the inside outward. Contrary to patriarchal voices, therefore, erotic desires are not inherently selfish or antithetical to moral value. Progressive seekers of justice-love can well imagine living by an ethical eroticism that enjoys life's pleasures and at the same time prods us to pursue a more ethical world. The erotic can fuel our passion for justice. It invites us to take ourselves *seriously* as sexual persons, *playfully* as erotic equals, and *persistently* as those who refuse to accept oppression as the way things must be. Defenders of the status quo rightly see erotically empowered people as dangerous and beyond their control.

Guiding Principles for an Ethical Eroticism

An ethical eroticism operates with four central value commitments: to honor the goodness of the body, of bodily integrity or self-direction, of mutuality, and of fidelity. Each of these contributes to erotic justice within intimate and all other social relations.

To begin with, bodies are good, capable of giving and receiving plea-sure. Our bodies deserve respect and care. As Carter Heyward explains, "the body is to be taken with ultimate seriousness. There is nothing higher, nothing more holy."[12] Moreover, sex is good. Sexual touching expresses our moral power to love and care for each other through our bodies. Sensuous touching, sometimes genital and sometimes not, com-municates our regard for each other in powerful yet gentle ways.

Bodily integrity or self-direction is a basic moral good. Each person is entitled to choose whether (and how) to relate with his or her body. Body right means freedom from control and manipulation by another, as well as having the power to direct the use of one's body and body space accord-ing to context and one's own choices.

Ownership of a person's body and, by extension, of the person's self has been a historic principle of racist patriarchy. The conventional mar-riage ethic promotes male ownership of women but mystifies its control of women and children by romanticizing family life. Honoring bodily integrity disqualifies, without exception, the right to possess or exploit any person's body space. Another's body is not mine for the taking, nor do I give up my right to my own body either when I consent to have sex with someone or once we have had sex together. Body right requires that we respect each other as persons and, therefore, as whole body-selves. As John Stoltenberg warns, "You may or may not love—but you must always respect. You must respect the integrity of your partner's body. It is not yours for the taking. It belongs to someone real."[13]

Morally sound sexual relations also depend on, and aim for, mutuality. Sex is not doing something *to* someone else, but is rather a mutual process of *being with* and *feeling with* another person. Persons, not mere body parts, meet and touch. An ethical eroticism requires paying attention to the other person as if to oneself. Both parties must show up, and be accounted for, together.

Good touch, it should be emphasized, requires consent. Consent is valid only if each party has the right (and the power) to exit, without penalty, from any interaction. Consent is actualized in relations of mutual respect, in which parties share a common, though rarely an equivalent, vulnerability, that is, a capacity to be affected by the interaction. Mutuality is a dynamic, open-ended process in which each person is empowered to give to, as well as to receive from, the relationship in a fair, nonexploit-ative manner. In a mutually structured relation, both parties experience themselves as cared for and respected.

Finally, fidelity makes durability, substance, and hope possible within relationships. Fidelity means honoring our commitments, working together to maintain trust, and renegotiating with one's partner as needs, desires, and conditions unfold. Fidelity is dependent on mutual openness and honesty. It is violated by dishonesty, but also by an unwillingness to grow and change as the relationship develops. The precise requirements for fidelity cannot be prescribed in advance or in a legalistic, static fashion, but should be assessed in terms of what best honors the needs of both parties and the integrity of the relationship itself. This is difficult in an erotophobic culture, both fearful of and fixated with erotic power and sexuality. Erotophobia promulgates not only hatred of the body but also deep self-hatred, so we therefore are enculturated not to name our needs forthrightly. Our socialization in a racist patriarchal culture frustrates our desire to be rightly connected, but—wonder of wonders—our imaginations help us envision alternative ways of loving beyond the limited roles the culture has assigned us.

These values undergird an ethic that is sex-affirming and respectful of erotic power as a moral resource. Special controls on sexuality are not necessary, nor do we need fear-based strategies to restrain erotic power. A mature sexual ethic focuses not on what must be prohibited or kept under control, but rather on the quality of relationship, the pattern of respect and care, and how power is distributed and expressed. It also does not lose sight of the fact that the interpersonal is connected to, and dependent upon, the social and cultural matrix in which our lives are embedded. We need an erotic ethic that appreciates how the personal and sociocultural are intertwined, but that also knows how justice makes love more pleasurable and therefore more desirable in all aspects of our lives.

An Ethic That Eroticizes Justice

Coming of age in regard to sexuality requires celebrating, not simply tolerating, a rich diversity of sexual relationships that have moral substance. Celibacy and heterosexual marriage are valued insofar as they are freely entered into and enhance people's dignity and well-being, but marriage and celibacy do not exhaust the full range of morally acceptable options. A mature Christian ethic does not restrict sexual activity to marriage alone. Nor does it bless all sex within marriage as morally acceptable. Widespread patterns of coercive sex within marriage, including marital rape, are sufficient reason for discarding highly romanticized notions about the sanctity of the marriage bed.[14] Only those sexual relations, marital and nonmarital, that exhibit mutual respect and genuine care for the partners should be celebrated by the wider community.

The prevailing sexual ideology diminishes human loving, both in scope and beauty, by making heterosexual coupling compulsory. Heterosexual monogamy is regarded as the necessary and "naturalized" arrangement, within a gender hierarchy, for a man and a woman to find their "significant other" who will complement, and therefore complete, their genderized half-identities. Compulsory coupling has several ethically significant consequences. First, if long-term coupling is the only arena for sexual expression, then many people are left entirely out of consideration. Conventional sexual ethics for the most part have paid insufficient attention to the sexuality of single persons.[15] Single persons have been assumed to lack sexual needs altogether or else have been expected to repress their sexuality by remaining celibate, even over the course of a lifetime. On the one hand, then, single persons have been desexualized. On the other hand, they have been oversexualized and viewed with fear and suspicion as potential threats to intact couples.[16]

Second, compulsory coupling also encourages dependency patterns between intimates. As social ethicist Mary Hobgood explains, the idealization of romantic love encourages both men and women to locate that one special person who supposedly can meet all their intimacy needs. This directs them to look outside themselves for fulfillment. "We are thereby taught," Hobgood observes, "to abdicate responsibility for ourselves."[17] Because their "missing half" controls their happiness, people fail to take responsibility for their own happiness or to pursue their own sense of what brings them satisfaction. In addition, compulsory monogamy restricts the range and significance of other friendships. As a couple, people are discouraged from establishing emotionally strong connections outside their twosome. A highly restrictive monogamy ethic, therefore, weakens ties with the larger human community. Couples turn inward and become increasingly isolated from other socially meaningful, emotionally satisfying relationships. An enormous burden is placed on two people, and on them alone, to provide the emotional depth and sociality that only a diverse community can offer.

This marriage ideology fits neatly with, and is reinforced by, the dominant capitalist ethos that patterns all relationships as property relations. In a capitalist patriarchy, men exercise the right of property ownership, especially over female partners. The fiction of a scarcity of love further justifies competition for establishing monopoly control over another person as one's personal "supply." Capitalist ideology also reinforces the prevailing antisexual, erotophobic ideology by positing that the desire for pleasure leads inexorably to narcissistic self-indulgence.

A liberating ethic must insist, quite to the contrary, that viewing our social ties as property relations, in which some seek possession of others, distorts intimacy and blocks real pleasure. Authentic pleasure emerges only as people belong securely to themselves as persons in their own right and as they then relate to others out of strength and personal integrity, rather than from an inner emptiness. A real self can meet another as a real self. As Hobgood comments, "Love, including married love, thrives only as mutual recognition and passionate connection between two distinct selves fully capable of healthy self-love and personal satisfaction in their separate lives."[18]

Sexual ethics traditionally have focused more on the *form* than on the *substance* of sexual relations. Conformity to prevailing social expectations about entering marriage (or reentering marriage after divorce) has been the primary criterion for personal maturity and social responsibility. Substantive questions have been downplayed or ignored, especially moral concerns about safety and consent, commitment, and the distribution of power. Similarly, the conventional taboo against same-sex sexual activity has focused on the gender of the sexual partners rather than on the moral quality of their relationship. Following the logic of a patriarchal ethic, people tend to fixate on the question of whether loving, same-sex relations can be morally acceptable. Meanwhile, morally dubious activities, such as rape within "respectable" marriages, escape scrutiny altogether. Conventional sexual ethics have not been sufficiently discriminating.

Patriarchal logic is no substitute for informed ethical judgment. Once we question the normativity of compulsory heterosexuality, it no longer makes sense to validate heterosexual relations merely because they are heterosexual or to discredit same-sex relations because the love expressed is between two women or two men. It no longer makes sense to condemn nonmarital sex simply because it falls outside a particular formal, institutional arrangement. Our ethical sensibilities must be realigned. For too long, the moral problematic has been misnamed, especially in churches, as the "problem" of homosexuality and nonmarital sex. Granted, gay, lesbian, and bisexual persons and sexually active singles enjoy an apparent freedom by establishing their relationships outside the structure of patriarchal marriage. A justice hermeneutic, however, allows us to see that the moral problem does not lie in nonconformity to patriarchal norms of sexuality. Rather, the problem of sexuality is reflected in our society in the large number of loveless, graceless relationships of all kinds, heterosexual and homosexual, marital and nonmarital, and in the splitting off of eroticism from mutuality. The crisis is grounded in the widespread devaluing of women, of gay/lesbian/bisexual people, and of persons in nondominant racial/ethnic communities.

This moral crisis is only made worse by the refusal of religious communities to challenge compulsory heterosexuality, as well as gender, class, and race supremacy. Reaching a new maturity about these matters will require honoring gay men, lesbians, and bisexual persons of all colors in the life and leadership of churches. It will also require public celebration of same-sex relationships, including same-sex marriages, as fully embodying covenantal love between two people. Furthermore, a trustworthy ethic will not seek to control people by fear and guilt, but rather will equip them to make responsible decisions and live gracefully, even in the midst of failure and ambiguity.

By now it should be obvious why neither marriage nor heterosexuality, but *justice in sexual relationships* should be morally normative. A commitment to justice affirms our common decency amid the diversity of human sexualities and honors our shared need for intimacy and affection. As sexual persons, we experience a quite remarkable yearning for communion with others, the natural world, and God. This yearning is at once emotional, cognitive, physical, and spiritual. Sexual passion for connection and communion ennobles our lives. Only by unabashedly reclaiming sex as intrinsic to Christian (and other forms of) spirituality can we begin to recapture a more earthy, sensuous appreciation of how we are created to be justice-lovers, relishing pleasure and mutual affirmation. Staying in touch with our senses, with one another, and with whatever moves us in delight, horror, or curiosity, is an open-ended moral project full of surprises and challenges.

For this reason, it is fitting not to grant special status to heterosexual marriage, but rather to celebrate all sexual relations that deepen intimacy and love. Marriage is valued, but not because it serves as a license for sex or establishes ownership rights over another human being. Rather, egalitarian, justice-bearing marriages offer a framework of accountability and a relatively stable, secure place in which to form durable bonds of mutual trust and devotion. Marriages should deepen friendship beyond, as well as within, the primary relation and avoid fostering patterns of dependency and control.

Some marriages make room for additional sexual partners. Others thrive only by maintaining sexual exclusivity. Although justice requires relational fidelity, the precise requirements of this fidelity cannot be determined in advance. Rather, the concrete "terms of endearment" can be refined only as a particular relationship develops. For some people, the covenant bond will most likely be violated not by satellite friendships or "outside" sexual friendships, but rather by refusals to keep faith and give priority, within a multiplicity of relationships, to the marriage commitment. For all people, fidelity requires an ongoing willingness to respond fairly and forthrightly to the demands of the relationship.

Obviously, what I call justice-bearing marriages require a high degree of moral responsibility, mutual commitment, and willingness to respect the diversity of each partner's needs. Equally, same-sex couples should have the right to participate in and receive community support for an enduring, formalized sexual partnership. For all couples the question becomes: When is their union properly "consummated," and how do they (and others) know that? Sexual activity alone does not mark the establishment of a marriage or an authentic sexual friendship, nor should it. Sex does not "make" a marriage happen. Neither does a religious ceremony nor authentication by the state. Since the church does not make a marriage happen but rather offers a blessing, we need to clarify appropriate criteria for knowing when a marriage actually occurs.

Marriages take place only as persons are wholeheartedly committed to each other as genuine equals and thereby experience mutual respect, care, and affection. At least some divorces signal less an end to a marriage than a public announcement that no genuine marriage had ever taken place. In order to mark the moral significance, therefore, as well as the riskiness, of marriage as a sustained moral commitment, religious communities should be more discriminating about which relationships to bless and when to bless them. At the same time, the blessing of relationships should never become a way to reassert ecclesiastical control or to police people's lives. Rather, public celebrations should highlight the way a faith community honors the moral integrity of its various members and their diverse relationships. As biblical scholar William Countryman notes, "the church would perhaps be better advised not to solemnize marriages at the inception of the relationship itself, but to wait a period of some years before adding its blessing."[19] Then at last religious people might get it right: Neither sexist nor heterosexist unions are "made in heaven."

An ethic of erotic justice *celebrates the plurality of friendship and intimacy needs and respects differences* within a variety of partnership forms, including heterosexual marriages with and without children, sexual friendships between consenting adults, shared living arrangements, and same-sex unions. It supports persons in exploring their own sexuality with tenderness and joy. It also encourages their respect for the sexualities of others. Appreciation of diversity is essential. Difference rather than uniformity, change rather than stasis, mark human sexuality, as well as our lives more generally—not only *among* persons and groups, but also *within* each individual's life. Few of us are the same today as we were in our teen years or in our twenties, forties, or sixties.

Thanks largely to the feminist and gay/lesbian/bisexual liberation movements, fewer people now hold to rigid notions of gender. We are stretching the boundaries of traditional gender roles and challenging patriarchal categories that limit erotic possibility to the narrowly constructed confines of "heterosexuality" and "homosexuality." These labels tell us very little about people's lives or the character of their love. Many people, male and female, have discovered new, often unexpected possibilities beyond such categorical confines. Many women, for example, report the delight of learning how to bring themselves to orgasm, thus shattering for themselves the myth of the frigid, nonorgasmic female who is dependent on the male for sexual gratification. Some heterosexual persons have found themselves erotically attracted to people of the same sex. The lesbian and gay communities include countless people such as myself who have lived formerly (and contentedly) as self-identified heterosexuals. The culture's prevailing gender and sexual categories have never adequately described and in fact have seriously distorted, the complex meanings of our lives. These constructs distract people from what genuinely matters.

Living comfortably with change and ambiguity requires maturity and a willingness to delight in difference and novelty. It also requires confidence in our collective ability to make meaningful moral distinctions and responsible choices. Religious communities should not be policing people's sex lives, but rather educating them about this real world of sexual diversity and expanding their moral imaginations.

A liberating ethic of erotic justice encourages compassion and invites people to *learn from failure*. Failure is not the end of possibility. People sometimes gain moral insight by failing, making corrections, and moving on. An ethic of grace is not an excuse for irresponsibility. Rather, it welcomes the possibility of new beginnings, of recovering from ill-considered choices or painful experiences, and of retaining a sense of oneself as a responsible person whose task is not to achieve perfection, but to "do the best one can" in light of real limits and sometimes forced options.

A justice ethic recognizes that it is immoral to withhold from people knowledge of their own bodies. Attempts to prevent teenage pregnancy, for example, by prohibiting sexual experimentation or by instilling guilt and shame about sex are both inappropriate and counterproductive to young people's developing moral discernment and decision-making skills. Like adults, teenagers need an ethic of empowerment rather than control. They need access to accurate, reliable information about human sexuality. They need encouragement to explore their own values and needs in a nonjudgmental, supportive environment. They require recognition of their self-worth and ability to make genuinely life-enhancing decisions. Teens must also be credited with the fortitude to deal with the consequences of their choices.

For people of all ages, becoming more responsible about sexuality must include learning how to assert one's own needs while respecting others' body right. It also means sharing insights, skills, and quandaries with others and, above all, being willing to risk being vulnerable and asking for help. Breaking the silences around sex not only dispels myths and misinformation. It encourages us to ask critical questions. It helps us bolster one another and reject unjust cultural norms. It may also empower persons, young and old, to resist abuse and claim their right to safety and bodily integrity.

An ethic of erotic justice *from the start rules out relations in which persons are abused, exploited, and violated.* People must be empowered to protect themselves from abuse and exploitation, from uninvited touch and coercive sex. Perpetrators of sexual violence and abuse must be held accountable. They must be encouraged to alter their behavior, as well as to make restitution to those they have harmed. At the same time, social structures that breed inequality and violence must be challenged. People also need protection from disease and unintentional pregnancy. In an age when sexually transmitted disease, including HIV infection, is spread epidemically, it is incumbent on all sexually active persons to know their health status and not place themselves or others at risk for infection. Acting "as if" one is HIV-positive and consistently observing safer-sex guidelines is one strategy that allows for a healthy and active sex life and, importantly, keeps the focus on the disease, not the sexual activity, as the appropriate cause for concern.

An adequate sexual ethic does more than insist that no harm be done to others. It *strengthens people's well-being and self-respect.* Good sex is good because it touches our senses powerfully but also because it enhances our self-worth and deepens our desire to connect more justly with others. The key concerns of this ethic are how power is shared and the quality of caring. Sex is not something one "does to" another person or "has happen" to oneself. Rather sexual intimacy is a mutual process of feeling with, connecting to, and sharing as whole persons. We enhance our sense of self-worth by attending with care to what is happening to the other person as well as to ourselves. In the midst of sexual pleasuring with a partner, we do not "lose" ourselves as much as we relocate ourselves in the in-betweenness of self and other, as we receive and give affection and energy.

Body respect and pleasuring can teach us how wrong it is to regard all self-interest as morally tainted. As lovers and friends, we can be rightly interested in our *mutual* enjoyment and well-being. Being interested in others does not detract from, but complements our self-interest, and vice versa. What harms or diminishes another can never be good for me. Positively stated, whatever enhances another's well-being also deepens the quality of my life. In a culture that confuses love with controlling others (or with giving power over to another), religious communities should educate us to trust, deep within our bodies, that we connect with others only to the extent that we stay genuinely present to, and affirming of, ourselves. Self-awareness means monitoring our feelings and, with as much consistency as possible, honoring an obligation to honor ourselves as well as the other person.

An ethic of erotic justice, therefore, *does not lower but raises moral expectations*. It teaches us to demand for ourselves (and others) what we deserve, namely, to be whole persons to each other and to be deeply, respectfully loved. A gracious, liberating ethic will teach us to claim our right to erotic justice and also to invest in creating a more just and equitable world. In our late-capitalist culture, desire has been commodified to sell goods. In that process of commodification, desire has been narrowly sexualized and privatized, so much so that for many people erotic desire now denotes only desire of a genital sort. More specifically, desire has been truncated to mean taking pleasure in possession. Possessiveness is a primary virtue in a capitalist political economy. Pleasure has become the pleasure of owning consumer goods and status objects, as well as exercising monopoly control over another person as "my man" or "my woman." It is a major challenge to enlarge the meaning of desire to incorporate once again a sense of being free-spirited, full of joy in being alive and "non-possessed," throughout one's life. This expanded notion of desire can be a mighty, though tender, spark from within us, enlivening our desire for a more ethical world. Erotic power can stir us to engage in a full-bodied way in creating justice.

My suspicion is that the pervasive fear of sex and passion, rampant in all patriarchal religious traditions, is deeply implicated in the difficulty many people have in sustaining an interest in, much less a passion for, social justice. By and large, even liberal Christians either regard patriarchal control as socially necessary or dismiss sexuality as a rather indifferent matter that bears little consequence compared to "larger," more "legitimate" social issues. For many people, the link between sexuality and justice is muddled at best. By not paying attention to sexual oppression, people fail to grasp how a multiplicity of interconnected social oppressions operate in the small and large places of their lives, in and on their bodies and the body politic. These injustices diminish human loving. When people are willing to accept power as control in their intimate lives, they are also likely to acquiesce to other oppressive structures that control them. They fail to see that sexual oppression is intimately bound up with race, gender, and class oppression. People fail, therefore, to connect their personal pain with larger systemic patterns of injustice.

White, middle-strata Christians are deeply hurting but have few clues about the sources of their suffering. They project their fear and pain onto more vulnerable groups, including feminist women, people of color, and gay/lesbian/bisexual persons. Out of touch with their own bodies (and feelings), they are also distanced from the beauty and moral value of other body-selves, especially among the "culturally despised." They are at a loss about how to reclaim their personal power and zest for life. Tragically, when people are cut off from genuine community and when their physical and emotional needs are not being adequately met, they tend to become more repressive about sex, more judgmental about differences, and more unforgiving toward themselves and others. In the process they become dangerous. They turn their repressed anger and rage on the very people they ought to be listening to and learning from, the ones most insistent about the goodness of every body.

Moral Vision and Personal Courage

A final component of a justice ethic is, therefore, the *reclamation of moral vision and personal courage* to step out toward an alternative possibility. Nothing is more important than our capacity to imagine a radically different world. Such envisioning involves trust. We must trust that we are capable of far more than greed, violence, and sexual irresponsibility. We can imagine, and commit ourselves to, the creation of a radical new world in which all belong and no one's beauty is denied. At the same time, we need a simple yet morally urgent awareness that not everyone lives and struggles as we do. To imagine the actual life conditions of other people— whether the other is "other" by gender, sexual orientation, race, class, culture, age, or physical or mental condition—is indispensable for doing justice. Religious communities serve us well when they forthrightly criticize the "frozen horizon" of present arrangements. They should be helping to stir in us a more imaginative and more truthful picture of the richly diverse human community.

Reconstructing Christian sexual ethics requires our moving beyond liberal presuppositions which privatize love and disconnect justice from personal life. A social order in which sexism, racism, and economic exploitation are significantly reduced will be a social order in which love has a fairer chance of prospering among the amazing variety of human differences. Men will be better off if they treat women well. Males of all ages will no longer feel required to prove their "manhood" at all costs or falsely claim social superiority in all things. We will be able to rest more comfortably in our own skins as human beings with a full complement of strengths and weaknesses. White-skinned people may learn not to project our fears and anxieties onto darker-skinned peoples, but instead to gauge our humanity by our capacity to make friendships and express genuine solidarity across a wide social diversity. Respect, the valuing of other persons and oneself, is foundational for learning how to eroticize—"turn on" to—relations of equality and fairness, and how to take real delight in other people's company. Where there is mutual respect, admiration, and a desire to equalize relationships, in the bedroom and beyond, we can experience genuine ecstasy down to our toes. When we encounter each other in our differences and manage to express candor, good faith, and trust, we find something beautiful and powerful to our senses. This kind of respectful connecting is erotic, powerful, and good.

Loving well in the midst of cultural crisis means engaging passionately in doing justice, both close to our skins and at a distance. As we gain confidence in our capacity to reorder our relations toward mutual respect and care, it becomes more apparent that we do not need a distinct, separate ethic to regulate sexuality. Erotically empowered people do not need systematized rules and regulations to control and "cover their genitals." In fact, rigid rules and restrictions about sex only perpetuate body alienation and genital fixation. We must not forget that it is racist patriarchy that has posited eroticism as a wayward power requiring special controls to keep things safe and properly ordered. From a feminist and gay liberation perspective, however, what is needed is not a specialized code to regulate sexuality, but rather *an adequate life ethic* that can incorporate the erotic as an indispensable human power. Such a comprehensive ethic will delight in the incomparable value of people, insist on mutual respect as a basic social norm, and hold people accountable for their actions.

The fact is that we simply do not need a specific ethical code to regulate whether, when, and with whom to touch genitals. Rather, we need a more general, fluid, and dynamic *ethic of respectful touching*. This ethical approach will value the body's remarkable capacity to communicate powerful meaning, including love and affection, but it will address sexual activity as only one area for such communication between persons. This ethic's primary concern will be strengthening the practices of good touch and ending longstanding patterns of abuse and exploitation, especially of children, older adults, and other socially vulnerable people. Such an ethic will, at long last, allow us to give sex its due as an important, treasured aspect of our lives, but without reinforcing this culture's genital fixation. Sexuality will retain an importance, but not more importance than it deserves. The ethical focus will be on how people learn to negotiate and receive each other at the level of friendship and interpersonal intimacy.

A liberating ethic values the erotic as a resource for enriching life, from its most intimate to its most public aspects, but the notion of pleasure is expanded well beyond erotic stimulation between intimate partners. Pleasure is no longer reduced merely to "private pleasures." People also search for and find genuine satisfaction in nonalienated work, in schools that educate for critical consciousness, in raising children to be in touch with their feelings and self-worth, and in other life pursuits that move body and soul. At home in their bodies, people are more likely to enjoy being in the company of others.

In the next chapter I will examine how violence betrays people's trust and blocks intimacy in people's lives. The focus will be on men's violence against women, children, and marginalized men. Up to this point I have argued that the contemporary crisis of sexuality is primarily a *crisis in heterosexuality*, located in the sexist, racist ordering of social relations that legitimate male dominance and female subordination. To speak now more candidly, this moral crisis is primarily a crisis in *male* sexuality. A racist patriarchal code of compulsory masculinity distorts men's lives, their social connections, and their spirituality whether they are gay, bisexual, or heterosexual.

A contemporary Christian sexual ethic must address this crisis in men's lives at a deep level. How can men of all colors and sexualities embrace erotic justice as a way of life with women, as well as with other men? Blaming men or stigmatizing men is not the answer. Instead we must see in this crisis the opportunity for men in particular to face the radicality of injustice in our daily interactions, including our most intense personal relations. A liberating ethic holds out the hope that by facing the full scope of injustice we can find possibilities for moving forward toward justice and making a truly win-win situation possible among intimates—men and women, men and men, women and women. That possibility depends to a great extent on men's disenchantment with and willingness to *unlearn* the racist patriarchal ethos of ownership and control. Likewise, it also depends on our desire to *learn fairness anew*, to negotiate our needs with gentleness and good humor, and to take responsibility as powerful justice-lovers.

5

Securing the Sanctity of Every Body
Men Confronting Men's Violence

> I say we learn from what we have done and
> make choices to do better—for the sake of
> others and for the sake of our own best selves.[1]
>
> —John Stoltenberg

A liberating ethic of sexuality affirms the goodness of bodily pleasure, but it holds this affirmation in tension with another, equally important claim. For many people, sexuality is intertwined with violence, pain, and abuse. Guaranteeing the sanctity of each and every person, therefore, has moral urgency for those who regard bodily integrity as a fundamental moral good. It is also necessary to clearly differentiate between sexual intimacy on the one hand, and sexual coercion and control on the other. Without question we must condemn abuse and body violation as morally wrong, but that addresses only half the problem. We must also sustain a sex-positive ethical framework. Our challenge ethically is to find ways to be antiviolent without being antisex.

Maintaining a sex-positive stance is a daunting project. The pervasive sex-negativity floating so freely in this culture easily acquires an air of legitimacy in the name of opposing violence among intimates. Many people become sexually repressive out of their reasonable distress over sexual violence. They resort to shame, guilt, and self-hatred as strategies for keeping their own sexuality and that of others in line, safe, and under control. However, concern for safety, when separated from a sex-positive ethical stance, readily becomes a cover for re-introducing repressive control. Control not only inhibits loving intimacy but sets the stage for violence, degradation, and humiliation of others. In the name of decency and nonviolence, therefore, sex-fearing people, including many Christians, only reinforce the problem they hope to alleviate. The ethical challenge is formidable. We must insist upon respectful, nonviolent touching as a fundamental, nonnegotiable requirement in all contexts and for all social relations, genital and other-wise. Making this message credible is no small task within a culture that associates and frequently confuses pleasure and pain, sexuality and danger.[2]

Violence as a Men's Issue

As a gay man, I daily feel the enormous challenge to end violence against my own community.[3] I work with other gay, lesbian, bisexual, and transgender people and our allies to reduce the threats to our survival, but my concern about violence extends well beyond my immediate community's struggles. I am no less challenged *as a man* to look at sexual violence from the perspective of one who belongs to the male gender class in a male supremacist culture.

Two factors define sexual and domestic violence primarily as a men's issue. First, intimate violence is pervasive in this culture. In fact, what is perhaps most noteworthy about this violence is its very ordinariness. Violence has become a routine way of life, as demonstrated by the large numbers of reported, and even larger numbers of unreported, assaults on women, children, and less powerful men.[4] In their 1995 review of U.S. statistics, two criminologists, Piers Beirne and James Messerschmidt, point out that between two and six million wives are battered each year by their husbands and, further, that "according to the FBI, the rate of reported rape continues to rise. Since 1988 the number of rape offenses reported to the police has risen by 18 percent."[5] Moreover, interpersonal violence in some form takes place in roughly half of all intimate relationships. Women are the most likely victims, and when intimate violence occurs, victims are often confronted by violence in several forms. For example, "studies indicate that between 30 and 60 percent of all wife beating involves some form of sexual abuse."[6]

Other statistics paint an equally grim picture. One in four or, by some estimates, one in three women is sexually assaulted in her lifetime. One in seven married women is sexually assaulted by her husband or ex-husband.[7] In fact, wife rape is *more* common, not less common, than rape by strangers or acquaintances. Studies show that "the more intimate the relationship between the victim and the offender, the greater the chance that the rape attempt will be completed."[8] Domestic violence itself is the single largest cause of injury to women in the United States. Moreover, "the single most common occasion for female homicide is not robbery, gangs, or drugs, but an argument with a man."[9] By conservative estimates, 20–30 percent of girls now twelve years old, unless conditions change significantly, will be subject to violent sexual attack at some point in their lifetime. Among children, between one in five and one in three girls is vulnerable to sexual abuse. Estimates for boys run at least one in eleven.[10] The ordinariness of this violence is matched by its social invisibility, especially when the violence is directed against women of color or poor women.

A second fact of ethical concern is that men are overwhelmingly the agents of intimate violence. In the United States, statistics indicate that the vast majority (94 percent) of the victims of domestic violence are women. The vast majority of batterers (97 percent) are men.[11] Men also direct violence at other men in warfare, in assaults, in homicides, and in gay bashings.[12] In this society, therefore, a considerable number of men take on the role of victimizer, but another fact is less often discussed. In a racist patriarchal culture most men, like most women, fear men's violence, and for good reason. "Although there are a few reported cases of women raping men," as Beirne and Messerschmidt note, "males are relatively safe from sexual assault *unless they are in prison.*"[13] Male-dominated and male-segregated institutions and social settings are filled with violence, threats of violence, or fear regarding the outbreak of violence. Both men and women seek, therefore, to develop survival strategies in a variety of contexts in order to avoid male aggression.[14] Too often, however, people are left with the task of creating personal solutions to what is, more truthfully, a social problem of significant proportions.

The cultural equation of men with violence and of male sexuality with aggression is more accurate than most people, male or female, care to admit. As a man I ask myself, What must we do *as men*, across our differences of race, class, and sexual orientation, in order to make battering, sexual harassment, gay bashings, and rape the most shameful and unmanly things a man could do? How can we re-envision male sexuality and ground it more securely, as theologian Starhawk says, "in a body that can come fully alive only when it is no longer an extension of a weapon"?[15] This chapter specifically addresses men's work in disentangling male sexuality from violence, aggression, and abuse.

A Men's Movement against Violence

Whatever contributions men may make to this moral struggle, we stand in debt to the feminist liberation movement. Over the last two decades a grassroots feminist movement has identified male violence against women and children as a serious social problem. It has challenged public denial and indifference and created a hard-earned climate of belief about the nature and scope of domestic and sexual violence, including sexual abuse by clergy, therapists, and other professionals. Survivors have courageously come forward, refused to minimize their abuse or protect their offenders (even when a family member or trusted authority figure), and insisted on every woman's (and child's) right to safety. Their moral leadership guides the analysis and strategies of a broadbased social change movement to end violence in the bedroom, the family, and the social order, including the church.

A smaller, less visible profeminist men's movement has also emerged. It follows feminist analysis in identifying *men's* violence as the primary problem, calls for men's accountability to women, and agrees that women's (and children's) safety takes strategic precedence in efforts to curb sexual and domestic violence. The problem lies beyond the violence of individual men and rests, more broadly, in male supremacist power structures, along with the ideology that sanctions them. This profeminist, gay/lesbian-affirming, and antiracist men's movement assumes that progressive social change requires the critique of multiple, interlocking social structures of domination. Further, a progressive men's movement, if authentically liberating, must serve women's, as well as men's, interests in promoting a new social order in which the well-being of all persons can be firmly secured.

By putting victims' interests first, this profeminist men's movement violates racist patriarchy's norms. Not surprisingly, a second, *promale and antifeminist* men's movement has emerged in backlash against both the men's and women's liberation movements. This reactionary movement promotes "men's rights," that is, traditional male entitlements to dominance and privilege.[16] Because of this socially obstructionist movement, some feminists regard any kind of men's movement with a mixture of skepticism and hope. In *Women Respond to the Men's Movement*, Gloria Steinem remarks that, given the awful reality of antifemale abuse and men's general disinterest in social change, "we [women] both want to believe in male change, and have little reason to do so."[17] Some women fear that any men's movement will do only what men have always done, "blame women for their problems and defend their own privileges."[18] We must continually ask, therefore, whose interests are being served in any social movement? Are men's efforts to redefine masculinity making women safer? Are men doing the work necessary to transcend barriers of race, class, and sexual orientation among men, as well as between men and women?

A liberating ethic sees the root of men's violence not in (male) human nature, but in a hierarchical sociocultural system that makes dominant/subordinate relations normative for all human interaction and that encourages the socially strong to maintain superiority by force. As Susan Schechter notes, social domination, including male battering, is "individually willed, yet socially constructed."[19] Men who batter, rape, or engage in other forms of violence must be held accountable for their actions. But the problem of men's violence is far more extensive than those particular misdeeds by those particular men. A sociocultural system structured on inequities of gender, race, and class encourages (especially) white, hetero-sexual, affluent men to place themselves at the center of things and then expect others to do their bidding. Women's role as subordinates is to serve the needs of men, including fathers, husbands, clergy, employers, and male authorities generally. Male centrality—androcentrism—and men's distanc-ing from women and things associated with women are marks of hege-monic masculinity in this culture. Women and men alike have been socialized to accept this hierarchical system and the necessity of domina-tion in order to preserve social order.

A liberating ethic must be concerned with more than discrete acts of injustice, including acts of violence. It must also focus on social structures and their negative, dehumanizing impact on people. The fact that the overall social relationship between men and women is oppressive has consequences for the moral character of men and women. Participating in and benefiting from oppression warps men's characters and makes us fearful, distant, controlling, and rigid. Male gender privilege desensitizes us to injustice and allows us to evade full knowledge of our impact on oth-ers. "The distortion of males in macho-masculine culture," Rosemary Radford Ruether observes, "permits both a ravishing of relationships and an insensitivity to that ravaging."[20]

For example, men who batter their intimate partners are forceful but not powerful, or at least not powerful in any meaningful sense. Batterers wield coercive, unilateral power-over, but they are not powerful in the sense of exercising relational, moral power as power-with-and-for one another. Moral power sustains relationship with others. Each person is affected and humanized by the interaction.[21] Violent men, however, oper-ate not from a stance of being powerful and secure in themselves, but from powerlessness and fear of not being recognized as worthy. Paradoxically, a liberating ethic must therefore encourage men's *gaining power*, in the sense of enhancing their self-esteem and at the same time deepening their respect for others, especially women and children. Men need a strong sense of their inherent dignity as human beings. They need to claim their power to build relations that promote mutuality, not domi-nation and exploitation. We men need to trust, deep in our souls, that our lives are important, but we need also to sustain that moral knowing *in conjunction with* our knowing that women's lives are as important as our own. We share a common humanity.

Racist patriarchy maintains itself through external controls but also as the dominant group's values are internalized into the character structure of men and women alike. For men, masculinity is the character ideal that legitimizes social injustice. Males are socialized to acquire power-linked traits and to accumulate wealth, control, and status. If they fail, they are expected at least to control people subordinate to them in the social hierarchy. Men without status and power as well as men with status and power feel entitled to use whatever means are necessary, including violence, to assert their male prerogatives.

A nuanced social analysis is needed to discern real differences among men, as well as between men and women. For example, men who are socially marginalized by race, class, sexual orientation, physical or mental disability, and/or age are, like women, denied bodily integrity, self-direction, and social respect. More often than not, these men are *targets* of violence. They may also engage in horizontal violence against those likewise trapped in low-status, no-win positions. Because powerless men are taught like everyone else to hold powerless, vulnerable people in contempt, they often feel justified in relieving their pain by hurting others, especially when their targets are less powerful than themselves. Is it any wonder that men who have been deeply wounded in this culture also hurt others with regularity, especially when they fear being held in contempt for not being socially "on top" and masterful? The more people have been harmed by sexism, racism, economic exploitation, heterosexism, and the like, the greater the potential they have to "know" violence and to use it against themselves and others. Powerlessness corrupts, as does unilateral power-over.

In this society few men experience real power and control in their lives. In a capitalist economy that subordinates persons to their market value in generating profits, most nondominant men find themselves in a double bind of patriarchy's making: Men maintain self-respect by staying in charge of their surroundings, but at the same time they are expected to surrender control to social superiors without complaint. Since it is not safe to challenge more powerful men (or women), especially those with white-skin and class privilege, many men reassure themselves of their own superior manliness by seeking control over "their" women and children, those reasonably safe for them to abuse. Instead of addressing the real sources of their pain and powerlessness in the hierarchical social system, these men seek compensation in the form of "masculinity" and male privilege by lording over their partners and family members. In so doing they only alienate themselves further from those people most inclined to offer them love and support. Moreover, societal tolerance for male violence against women and children functions as a means of social control over men. Instead of protesting the social system which devalues them, many men twist their anger into rage at those nearest to them, the women and children in their lives who also lack power but who are culturally designated as "appropriate victims" of male control and domination.[22] Men's displaced violence serves, therefore, as a safety valve that preserves the status quo while reconciling these men to their own subordination in the capitalist political economy.

Male enculturation into dominant masculinity has at least three consequences. First, many men fail to notice or listen to others. They universalize their own experience as normative, presuming that women or at least other men share their outlook. Second, men and boys are easily convinced that what is good for them is also beneficial for social subordinates and will be well received by them. Finally, privileged men lack accurate knowledge about women, children, and nondominant men whom they dismiss as Other, that is, without essential (male) value and point of view. As a consequence, know-it-all men are deprived of consensual validation, the kind of ongoing feedback people must depend upon to understand and then correct their actions in response to what others tell them. For survival reasons, social subordinates know much more about social dominants than the latter even begin to know about those they discount, literally, as nobodies.

No matter how much power the racist patriarchal system gives any man, his power is useful only in keeping things going according to present rules. It does not make real change possible. When a man actively resists by deviating from the status quo, his power is taken away. For example, gay men who "come out" and visibly dissent from the normative sex/gender system, especially by standing in solidarity with women, risk loss of employment, family, social status, even life. In addition, they often lose credibility with other men. They are no longer viewed as trustworthy, "real" men.[23] As nonconformists to patriarchal norms, openly gay men become traitors to the male cause and therefore like women become targets of male anger and resentment.

Men's power to change comes not from the patriarchal system, but entirely from another source. The power to change grows out of resistance to injustice and the forging of respectful connections with others in order to create an alternative social possibility. That moral struggle, always personal and political, requires men's critique of the socially constructed ideology of masculinity that enlists us in oppressing others at the expense of our humanity. The bad news is that racist patriarchal ideology has to some extent molded us all. The good news is that neither men nor women are simply passive recipients of such ideological formation but can resist their socially assigned destinations. Our moral calling is to minimize our acquiescence to injustice by maximizing our resistance to it.[24] The challenge for a liberating ethics is to alter convincingly the definition of masculinity so that it no longer denotes superiority and violence, but rather turns real manliness into the capacity to value and embrace others as equals.

Men's freedom to experiment with new social options is due to the gap between the racist, patriarchal character ideal for men and our failure to match up to these normative expectations. Such freedom requires entering into solidarity with other men across differences of race, class, and especially sexual orientation. Solidarity between gay and nongay men is particularly challenging because gayness is a distinctive social marker used to distinguish (and reward) real men from losers. In our justice work, we men must intentionally choose nonconformity to patriarchy and take pride *in our failure* as patriarchal misfits. Such resistance takes many forms, including our willingness, regardless of our erotic preferences, to be identified publicly as gay men, that is, as queer and "unmanly" men. Bonding with other justice-loving men is important, but not if it is in the typical pattern of standing against women and things associated with women. Rather, our "unmanly," justice-centered bonding must be politically countercultural: a publicly visible, consistently respectful bonding with men who likewise reject compulsory hetero-masculinity and honor women as their full social equals.

Because patriarchy teaches men to seek male gender privileges and approval from other men, this kind of justice-bearing bonding among men most likely will bring us trouble instead. A liberating ethic, however, does not ask us to deny our personal power or embrace passivity. Rather, we are called to take more honest ownership of the social power we already have *as men* and to become directly accountable to those affected by our power, especially women and children. As Beverly Harrison insists, feminism calls for genuine strength in men as well as in women, a strength born of the power of their relationship as mutually respectful moral agents.[25] This power is *moral* power, not patriarchal power. Such power is a genuine blessing for men as we experience our self-worth in our ties with others. In losing one life, we gain another by engaging in justice-making.

Becoming morally powerful does not mean leaning on women to do our political or emotional work for us, nor does it mean taking charge of the feminist movement. Rather it means becoming faithful, strong, and credible allies to women and taking responsibility to work with other men to humanize our lives. In particular, I see three areas for men's work in breaking the association of male sexuality with aggression: (1) studying our sexualities as men with varying degrees of gender, race, and economic privilege and reclaiming our bodily integrity; (2) breaking our silence about men's abuse of power and learning how to support and confront other men as needed; and (3) taking the plunge to struggle proactively for a far different world, a world without male gender privilege and devoid of the violence that sustains male gender supremacy. What follows suggests a partial agenda men need to work together to refine. I address these remarks primarily to other men because this is our change agenda, but I welcome women in this process if only to hold us accountable for our words and, more importantly, our actions.

Studying Our Lives, Our Sexualities

As men we need to take our own struggles seriously. We also need to pay attention to how others perceive us. How are we and the world we have fashioned experienced by those less powerful in church and society? A good place to start is by examining the preeminently masculine occupation of war making.

Training to be a good soldier is a process of instilling macho-masculinity, an intensification of the patriarchal male's socialization process. Men are trained to be aggressive, emotionally detached, and compliant to authority. Men literally toughen up in order to be able to dominate people with minimal guilt or remorse. Toughening is necessary in warfare so that men will use violence willingly. Good soldiers inflict suffering, tolerate pain, and risk death on command.

Military training involves distancing from one's body and from others. During basic training a young recruit's insecurity about his manhood is systematically manipulated in order to link his sexuality with aggression. Because manliness is a quality to be achieved and, therefore, something that can be lost or never firmly established, men are threatened with basic insecurity about their worth in a male system that generates fear and self-doubt about one's ability to make the grade. To avoid becoming an "unreal man," that is, like a woman or like less powerful men, soldiers strive desperately to establish their superiority by proving their manhood.

Soldiers demonstrate their fitness for duty by exercising control, through violence if necessary, over their own bodies and bodily senses, but also over others' bodies and nature itself. One Vietnam veteran describes basic training this way:

> The primary lesson of boot camp, towards which all behavior was shaped, was to seek dominance. . . . All else was nonmasculine. . . . Recruits were often stunned by the depths of the violence erupting within themselves. Only on these occasions of violent outbursts did the drill instructor cease his endless litany of 'you dirty faggots' and 'Can't hack it little girls?' After a continuous day of harassment, I bit a man on the face during hand-to-hand combat, gashing his eyebrow and cheek. I had lost control. For

the first time the drill instructor didn't physically strike me or call me a faggot. He put his arm around me and said that I was a lot more of a man than he had previously imagined. In front of the assembled platoon [he] gleefully reaffirmed my masculinity.[26]

Doing violence, but more importantly, enjoying dominance, establish a man's credentials as a masculine male. However, the pressure is unrelenting not to fail at any point by showing oneself less than a real man. An "effeminate," nonaggressive male is someone whom any drill instructor would recognize as "you dirty faggot."

The ideologies of the military and masculinity are intertwined. Both are based on contempt for women and fear of homosexuality or, more accurately, fear of erotic and emotional intimacy between men. Homosexuality is loathsome because it represents a break with compulsory heterosexuality, the strongest, most familiar social control on sexual expression in this culture. As discussed in chapter 2, heterosexism insists that both men and women conform to patriarchically constructed gender roles within dominant/subordinate power dynamics. An elaborate social construction of human sexuality is built on two assumptions: on gender dualism, that there are fundamental differences and an unalterable inequality between men and women, and on gender hierarchy, that male superiority and control over women is natural and good. The military may begrudgingly tolerate sex between men if it remains closeted, secretive, and shameful. No allowance is made, however, for homoerotic affection, especially when publicly affirmed. The "don't ask, don't tell" military policy renders gayness or same-sex affection invisible, and therefore guarantees that no genuine challenge to masculinist norms will upset patriarchal social relations. The ban on (open) gays in the military is not about sex (after all, boys will be boys), but rather about power and the fear of what may happen if men are more interested in loving than in fighting each other.[27]

The military strenuously reinforces a heterosexist code by granting legitimacy to only certain configurations of power and social relationships. When men are on top, all is well in the patriarchal world. Men retain their membership in the male club by avoiding the realm, tasks, and concerns of women. Above all, men must avoid erotic desire for other men because that desire has been assigned exclusively to women. Men fail by not desiring their dominant role over women. They are then perceived as queer, that is, like women and all others without power and status. The patriarchal imagination can only envision win-lose relationships in which there is a "winner" and a "loser," a "top" and a "bottom."

The modern soldier as a killing machine bears striking resemblance to patriarchy's other cultural hero, *homo economicus*, the corporate executive who makes a killing in the market, deftly manages corporate takeovers, and arranges plant closings without serious consideration of the human and social costs. Both the military and corporate roles require an abstractionism or remoteness from reality that is characteristic of masculinist ethos. Taught to fear and repress feelings of pain and vulnerability, men literally lose connection with themselves and others. Among the consequences of body repression and disconnection, one analyst observes, is that "the man who kills from a distance, without consciousness of the consequences of his deeds, feels no need to answer to anyone or [even] to himself."[28]

In this regard the battlefield soldier and the corporate manager may not be so different from the convicted rapist. As recent sociological studies of incarcerated rapists indicate, a patriarchal construction of masculinity enables some men to justify rape and use sexual coercion in good conscience within a cultural climate that generally tolerates violence and, more particularly, accepts hostility toward women. Masculinism allows men to discount women's experience. Men are therefore cut off from the humanizing that proceeds only through everyday contact with, and accountability to, real persons in real relations where claim making is reciprocal. Because their moral frame of reference excludes women, men who rape consistently misinterpret how they appear to their victims. Too deficient in moral imagination to "take the role of the other" when that other is female, men who rape can neither see themselves as their victims see them, nor can they imagine how their victims feel. Disconnected from real social interaction, rapists are able to say such things as, "She felt proud after sex with me"; "Once we got into it, she was okay"; and "She enjoyed it and it was like she consented."[29]

Whether in the military, corporate boardrooms, churches, or the family, male gender supremacy, intersecting with racism and classism, renders women's own experiential reality inconsequential. Without a lived, empathetic connection with women, men lack or, more accurately, refuse the kind of consensual feedback that would show them how to correct their actions in light of the effect on others. Conformity to hegemonic masculinity blocks men's social empathy. It also deprives them of access to such emotions as shame, guilt, and embarrassment. These emotions are significant resources for keeping one's moral bearings. Among other things, they send body-mediated warning signals against committing unjust and violent acts. Male participation in women's oppression, by deforming men's moral character, allows violence to escalate without serious internal moral checks.

Dissociation from the body and from body-mediated feelings is at the root of men's insensitivity to the suffering they inflict. People are connected to the world in and through their bodies, and when they no longer experience bodily connectedness they lose touch with reality. As with men who batter, those not able to feel their own pain are more likely to inflict pain on others. In the process they may not know what they are doing or be alert to what is being done in their name, a situation frequently true in war.

How might we deal with emotional illiteracy among men? What would it mean to engage in a process of moral re-formation and to literally "come to our senses"? Philosopher Glenn Gray offers a provocative suggestion. The appeals of war will dissipate, Gray argues, only when men experience a radical inner change and undergo an emotional reorientation, a process of gaining genuine intimacy with self, others, and the natural order.[30] Physical proximity alone does not guarantee intimacy, as battered women can readily attest. Genuine relationality or a sense of deep connection is possible only as people let go of control, recover vulnerability (the capacity to touch and be touched), and take delight in one another's co-humanity.

Deepening our capacity for intimacy with women is critical for men's moral re-formation; so is developing friendship and intimacy with other men. Joseph Pleck has observed that "ultimately, men cannot go any further in relating to women as equals than they have been able to go in relating to other men as equals."[31] Examining issues of male intimacy—with fathers, children, friends, co-workers, and lovers—is especially needed because homophobia and heterosexism teach us that real men exercise power over other men, as well as women, and that closeness to other men—or to another man—signals effeminacy, loss of manhood.[32]

As a gay man I struggle, along with many other men, to redefine manliness in ways that challenge patriarchal norms in our everyday relationships with women and with other men. I find that one of the gifts of the profeminist men's movement has been the creation of intentional spaces for social experimentation among men. As men gather with other men, we explore friendship, risk nonaggressive touch, and practice gestures of care, nurture, and mutual respect that are not often expressed in ordinary social interaction among men. Because patriarchy assigns women to deal with matters of intimacy and emotional nurture, we men have largely depended on our women friends and female lovers to provide the personal support we are slowly discovering we can give to and receive from other men. In honoring our love for other men, which sometimes includes genital touching but usually does not, we also come to celebrate love for ourselves and our own bodies. In our growing self-acceptance, we find a personal power to live more securely, in touch with our own value and the value of others.

Regaining intimacy may also make it possible to reclaim the erotic in our lives. Embracing the erotic as a source of moral knowledge, as discussed in chapter 4, goes against the dominant culture's wisdom that men are associated only with the "higher" things of the mind and spirit, not with the body. Claiming the goodness of bodily sensuality challenges the patriarchal assumption that the passions are intrinsically corrupting and the necessity of the will's control over the nonrational body. "We have been raised to fear the yes within ourselves, our deepest cravings," Audre Lorde argues. When we internalize that fear and live outside ourselves, that is, by external directives and without the navigational aids of our internal knowledge and needs, we become intimidated—a people easy to manipulate. We seek approval from authorities outside ourselves and look for safety through conformity. However, when we begin to "live from within ourselves," Lorde suggests, "we begin to be responsible to ourselves in the deepest sense."[33] By honoring the power of the erotic as our creative energy and life force, men are invited, as feminists say, to "experience our experience" and live in alignment with what genuinely feels right and true to us as sensuous, feeling, self-directing persons.

Women and gay men, but especially women and gay men of color, are the designated carriers of the erotic in this culture. They are therefore frequently targeted with negative projections about body, sex, and sensuality. One of the best tests, then, of men's willingness to honor the body and the value of the erotic is how well gay and bisexual men are respected, listened to, and befriended as guides for living passionately *as men*.

Bodily intimacy among friends is a prime location to gain the strength—morally, spiritually, and physically—to resist injustice and oppression. Whenever gay men celebrate our love for male bodies as morally good, whenever we refuse to "disincarnate" ourselves, and whenever we insist on the integrity of our bodies no less than our spirits, I believe we may well embody—not perfectly, but in ways that challenge the dominant ethos—a moral wisdom about the erotic that helps us delight in, not betray, our unique, body-grounded identities. This moral wisdom is something our lesbian sisters in particular have long pressed us to appreciate and trust as a primary moral resource.[34] As men gain more confidence in discerning what is genuinely life-giving for us, we can also expect to deepen our appreciation for that same process in others.

Here is the challenge: In patriarchal capitalism, all self-directed human needs are denied or strenuously frustrated except those that have been cultivated to maintain the smooth functioning of the political economy. Enormous pressure is applied to discount one's feelings and comply with external guides. Many men put up with unsatisfying, dehumanizing jobs in exchange for the dubious satisfaction of being considered a real man who earns his keep and rules the roost when he gets home. This only illustrates how accepting our manly duty thwarts our living on the basis of our own deepest desires for right relation beyond racist patriarchal categories. When we fear and ignore the erotic, we are more likely to give our power over to external authorities and believe that they know what is life-giving for us. We lose our soul—that place deep within us where spirituality and sexuality connect—and our capacity for joy.

Whenever we are cut off from the sensuous wisdom of the body and from our feelings, our capacity is diminished to experience pain or joy. When we stay in touch with our passion for life, however, we are less inclined to suffer pain or inflict it on others. We become less willing to tolerate abuse. Recovery of body connectedness and our capacity for pleasure bears directly, therefore, on the problem of violence in this culture. As James Nelson observes, considerable research shows an intimate connection between peacefulness and the capacity for body pleasure and between violence and the suppression of body pleasure.[35] Crosscultural studies indicate a high probability of rape, battering, and other forms of violence within social structures that are hierarchical and highly stratified in terms of race, gender, and other differences.[36] Studying our lives and sexualities in order to increase body pleasure and connectedness is among men's first work to eliminate violence from our lives.

Breaking Men's Silence about Male Violence

Outside of a few educational settings and court-mandated counseling programs, men rarely gather to discuss how we are implicated in violence against women and children. When the subject is addressed, my experience has been similar to Tony Eardley's, that we are "often confused, defensive, self-doubting or self-hating and resentful. A challenge to sexual violence may itself produce a violent reaction."[37]

Men's silence about men and violence might be explicable if all men were indeed rapists or batterers. The fact that some men are does not explain our general reluctance to address this topic. Another explanation might be that men generally feel guilt and shame about male violence. As studies regularly indicate, however, men who are violent against women and children rarely if ever willingly take responsibility for their violence as *their* choice or express genuine remorse for their controlling actions. Or, again, the fact that women, not men, traditionally have been the group society relegates to bind up the wounds of victims may account for men's distancing from this issue, but I suspect there is a different reason.

As members of a patriarchal society, men fear isolation and rejection by other men. To speak candidly about male violence as a men's issue requires courage for any man who dares to hold himself *and other men* accountable. Because any departure from the dominant male role incurs costs, speaking out about male violence may generate fear of being repudiated as disloyal and unmanly by other men. For this reason the primary danger for most women may not be the particular men in her life or their potential for violence. Rather, women's danger exists in the pull experienced by all men, including those sympathetic to feminism, to engage in male bonding. Men protect each other from the consequences of their brutality. The ethical challenge is to encourage men to break ranks with racist patriarchy. We must develop alternative community with other men—and with women—on a basis radically different from contempt for women or social disdain for whatever appears weak and vulnerable.

Glenn Gray is helpful about this phenomenon of men closing ranks with other men in the context of war. "The most potent quieters of conscience," he writes, "are evidently the presence of others who are doing the same things," along with the awareness that the soldier is acting under orders from those superior to himself who have authorized his conduct and will answer for his behavior.[38] I would only add that individual men who abhor violence may keep silence out of fear. They may fear alienating other men but also fear being subjected to ridicule and other men's violence.

Social psychologists John Sabini and Maury Silver have studied the formation of moral conscience and what equips persons to challenge injustice. Moral drift, a weakening of ethical conviction and clarity of purpose, occurs whenever individuals become afraid to speak out and publicly object to abuse perpetrated by others. In a famous experiment, a model prison was set up and staffed by volunteers, each assigned to a role as prisoner or guard. Although many of the "guards" soon displayed acts of brutality toward their "prisoners," some men showed moral sensitivity and refrained from any abuse. These "good guards," however, never spoke out to reproach any of their comrades for their misconduct. As a consequence, the brutality rapidly escalated. As Sabini and Silver conclude, "the failure to establish publicly the wrongness of a particular action gives it an implicit legitimacy." The lesson here is that the public establishment of a moral consensus among men that violence against women, children, and vulnerable men is unacceptable may not, by itself, restrain or inhibit such abuse. However, "at the very least, the *failure to condemn* allows those who ignore simple moral requirements to do so more easily."[39]

We men do violence by our silence as well as with our fists. Men who batter their female partners, for example, believe that other men support them in their right to control and discipline women.[40] It is important for us to communicate in visible, outspoken ways that male abuse is unacceptable behavior and will not receive even our tacit endorsement. As men, we need to alter the norms regulating male culture so that, first, men's violence is redefined as unmanly and, second, holding each other accountable becomes standard. Moreover, we must model publicly and privately our enthusiastic support for the empowerment of women as subjects of their own lives. We must vigorously defend women's and children's rights to bodily integrity, safety, and freedom from unwarranted control and from coercion and abuse.

If we accept our responsibility to work with other men; if we critique masculinism; and if we join with women in a broadbased social protest movement to end male violence, then the prevailing moral climate may finally shift. Abuses of male power should no longer be minimized or posited as simply aberrations on the fringes of an otherwise benign social system. The violence *in* a racist patriarchal system is fostered by the violence *of* a racist patriarchal system. Developing a public consensus that men's violence is wrong and will not be tolerated or excused may not accomplish all that needs doing, but it is a significant step in the right direction.

Another lesson for men who work on ending men's violence is a warning "not to go it alone." We must connect with others for support and mutual empowerment. Together we must find ways to break the silences, name and analyze the violences we know and participate in, and develop effective change strategies. All the while we must hold ourselves accountable to women and marginalized men regarding how our power affects them. For white men this will require learning accountability, that is, concrete answerability to women and men of color. For heterosexual men, this will mean listening to, learning from, and taking direction from gay men, bisexual persons, and lesbian women. For adults, it requires respecting the voices, as well as the needs, of children (and older and incapacitated persons as well).

For this change to work, we must understand that power for renewal and transformation is found in the collective, shared power to enlarge community and make it more just. The lone warrior, even the most courageous moral crusader, is too easily intimidated, isolated, or becomes burnt out. Even if he avoids these obstacles, the isolated male crusader too often believes he has all the answers, should be in charge, and has a right to exercise power-as-control rather than an obligation to act in-solidarity-with his peers. This man becomes counterproductive and a drain on energies because, in the guise of a "good guy," he actually replicates stereotypic macho-masculinist patterns.[41]

Another lesson is this: Men who personally reject the use of violence but do not engage in educating and when necessary confronting other men remain untrustworthy allies in the justice struggle. Being primarily concerned about one's own personal purity or one's status as a "good guard" in the midst of brutality does little to alter the conditions that perpetuate violence. Gay men experience similar behavior from liberal, nongay men who boast of being tolerant of homosexuality, but fail to speak out against homophobic behavior exhibited by their male associates. In fact, the presence of a few "good guards" helps to legitimize the prison system as a decent, even reasonable place. For many men, the personal too often becomes the *apolitical*. As a counterbalance, we need to develop analysis that connects our personal struggles with larger social justice commitments. We must appreciate how the problem of male violence is not limited to individual men, but is inextricably tied to the structural, organizational, and cultural arrangements that maintain an entire system of male power and privilege.

Because we are born into a social structure of domination we participate, willingly or not, consciously or not, in the violences that permeate our world. Where systemic injustices prevail, no one has clean hands. Just as in a white racist society it is false for white-skinned people to regard themselves as "above race" or nonracist, so in a violent society it is impossible, at least for men, to be nonviolent. The institutions we maintain by our well-meaning "manly" silence and by our social conformity to "the way things are" do the violence for us. For men of conscience, our struggle is to become *unmanly men* of peace with justice, passionately and visibly *anti*racist, *anti*violent, and *anti*patriarhal.

Radical individualism tempts us into misreading social reality by focusing only on discrete acts of hatred and violence as morally wrong. We fail to pay attention to how these actions are shaped and given their meaning by the larger sociocultural context. That context, as well as discrete acts of violence, require moral evaluation and response. Fortunately, "it is neither possible nor necessary," as Barbara Smith reminds us, "to be morally exempt in order to stand in opposition to oppression."[42] What is necessary is our resistance. We must join in a principled manner with others to be fully accountable for the use, misuse, and nonuse of whatever power we possess.

The starting point for men's justice advocacy is to engage in what John Stoltenberg calls "revolutionary honesty." We must commit ourselves to a painful yet necessary process of "telling the truth about male power, speaking the truth to male supremacy and starting with our own lives."

We privileged white men know more about the workings of male gender supremacy than we ordinarily admit. "As men," Stoltenberg writes, "we know more than we've ever really disclosed about how men keep women down, how men use race hate and sex hate to feel superior, how men despise 'faggots' in order to feel masculine."[43] Therefore we can explore the contours of this knowledge in order to transpose male gender privilege into a resource for liberation ethics as we analyze male gender supremacy from the inside out.

Such analysis and self-criticism will likely generate strong feelings among men. Telling our stories as men, especially of our complicity in violence against women, will likely generate among some men feelings of shame and remorse. These feelings, uncomfortable as they may be, should be welcomed because, as Stoltenberg notes, they provide a "powerful means of self-knowledge, of knowing in one's heart the deep connection between one's own acts and other human selves."[44] Shame and remorse are body signals that catch our attention and tell us that our wrongful actions require correction from us. Knowing that one has been hurtful and registering that awareness deep in one's soul is painful. It is also liberating. We may also acknowledge that we have chosen at other moments to do something right and respectful of others. These feeling-signals offer indispensable moral guidance.

Pride as well as shame is a valuable moral resource for men, but not all pride is liberating. Pride founded upon reified notions of male gender superiority is oppressive. The masculinity sustained by dominance is a false masculinity, not worthy of our interest. Such distortions rise out of an insecurity about one's worth, and insofar as men accept patriarchal logic, they will seek to fix their wounded selves by striving to establish their superiority in all things and over all others. From a liberating perspective, however, men's pride should reside not in false claims to superiority, but rather in being men who challenge oppression and hold ourselves accountable for our moral choices. Such integrity includes an ongoing willingness, developed and tested over time, to welcome constructive critiques from others about one's oppressive attitudes, actions, and passivity in the face of injustice.

As men we must examine our own lives. We must also ask women, children, and less powerful men how they view us. Do we in fact elicit fear and suspicion, or do we inspire confidence that we are men who show respect, fairness, and who work collaboratively? Our active listening and cooperation will depend, to a great extent, on our being secure in our self-worth and claiming our authenticity as men passionate about justice. As feminist theorist and political activist Charlotte Bunch observes, "successful coalitions are not built on feeling sorry for others or on being apologetic about one's existence. Coalitions are built around shared outrage over injustice."[45] Men, as well as women, have contributions to make—by generously sharing our moral wisdom, our righteous anger about injustice, and our passion for a new world.

Taking the Plunge into Justice

One challenge for justice-committed men, issued by feminist theologian Rosemary Radford Ruether, is to acknowledge the injustice of our own historical privilege as males and to recognize how the prevailing economic, political, and social structures and cultural ideologies, including the ideology of masculinity, keep male gender privilege in place.[46] I agree with Ruether's assessment, but I believe there is a second, related challenge. Men must not only publicly acknowledge their social privileges, but must also find creative ways to use that privilege to make justice happen and, whenever possible, reduce unearned advantages. Men can, for example, use their membership in the male gender class to gain access to other men whose assumptions and actions need challenging. We can confront the ways we and they avoid accountability to women. We can begin collectively altering those aspects of male culture that sustain woman-hating and other social hostilities.

If our access to other men is to be politically valuable, we must speak clearly in a profeminist, woman-positive voice. There is a bittersweet irony here. Men who often ignore women's naming of injustice will sometimes listen to other men. Men will listen especially to men of their own race and class because these men are significant others to them. As a male activist in the antirape movement observes, "Men are not used to listening to women in the same way we listen to men. Most of the men we talk with barely know how to listen to and hear anyone other than themselves. Rape is one measure of how poorly men listen to women."[47]

Perhaps most men will not take women seriously until social power, including economic resources, is more nearly equalized between men and women. Within a culture of gender inequality, male gender privilege blinds many men from noticing women or paying attention to women's moral claims. The same can be said about class, race, and heterosexual privilege. For this reason, the proactive doing of justice, as an open-ended process of correcting distorted power relations, may well become a precondition for enhancing moral responsiveness among men.

The positive use of male gender privilege as a resource for liberating ethics is illustrated by men's organizations working primarily with men to end rape and other violences. For example, Men Stopping Violence is a men's activist collective that educates men about sexual assault, critiques rapist attitudes and behaviors, and empowers men to resist sexist and racist socialization. Such work follows a feminist critique of "masculinization" as enculturation into violence and domination. At the same time, male antiviolence activists refuse to beat up on men. Profeminist men maintain empathy for and positive identification with other men. A complex awareness is needed. There is no doubt, on the one hand, that men do violence routinely against women. On the other hand, men can learn to live, and live well, without dominating others or resorting to violence.

Our humanity as men has been distorted and diminished because of our historical capitulation to sexism, racism, heterosexism, and other injustices. Restoring our moral integrity, especially for those of us with social privilege, is dependent upon our plunging enthusiastically into the work of justice, for our benefit and the benefit of others, and doing so with passion, intelligence, courage, and good humor.

The moral challenge for men is this: Stop blaming; take responsibility for our life choices; and, in an ongoing way, hold ourselves accountable for our power. Our power as men will be welcomed and not feared, however, only if it is consistently used to critique and dismantle racist, patriarchal privilege and make justice happen in the large and small places of our lives, including the bedroom, the workplace, church, and school.

Insofar as we actively seek women's critical feedback, desire to learn from others not like us, and direct the men's justice movement in ways that affect all our lives for the better, then we should also take pride—and delight—in being men of a certain stripe: men who have chosen well to break ranks and become energetic, passionate advocates for sexual and other kinds of justice all the days of our lives.

Conclusion

Reveling in an Erotic Spirituality of Justice

> This capacity for resistance, this longing for freedom
> is the holiest thing I know, in myself and in others.[1]
> —Melanie Kaye/Kantrowitz

Body-fearing theologies are dangerously out of touch with the energy and moral wisdom that come from extending justice to all persons, ourselves included. We need to become more aware of this reality and let it thoroughly inform our theological and ethical thinking. Control, coercion, and rigidity are the legacies of racist patriarchal Christianity. None of this gladdens the heart or lifts the spirits. Quite the contrary. The moral challenge before faith communities is this: They must choose whether to perpetuate an ethic of sexual control and body alienation or become committed to an erotic ethic that respects sexual diversity and insists on full mutuality between women and men, women and women, and men and men.

In our time, spiritual renewal is intimately bound up with justice-making and embracing the body as sacred, inviolate territory. Complicity in sexual injustice, including disparagement of erotic power, discredits moral authority and religious truth claims. About these matters, those of us who identify with Christian tradition will never be trusted as reliable guides until we make a decisive, irrevocable break with racist patriarchal Christianity. To become trustworthy, we must adopt a liberationing commitment to erotic justice.

To repeat an earlier point, our credibility as moral agents depends on our identifying *sexual injustice, not sexuality, as the moral problem* in this culture. We must make clear our commitment to reverse sexism, racism, heterosexism, and economic exploitation and to redress these injustices that have distorted human sexuality. We must insist publicly that sexual entitlement—the right to love and be loved—is a foundational moral right for all persons, without distinction. We must help people explore their sexuality with tenderness, as well as help them accept ongoing accountability for the impact of their actions on others. And we must unabashedly promote pleasure and the enjoyment of sensuality. This kind of decisive rupture with Christian erotophobia is necessary. Otherwise, for many the word Christian will continue to be associated with body hate, woman hate, and gay hate.

A compelling vision of the human good that includes sexual well-being is a moral vision that resonates with the best of religious values. As progressive people of faith, our calling is to embody *justice-love*,[2] an intimate co-mingling of our longing for personal well-being in our bodies and right-relatedness with others throughout the social order. For those who discount the intimate partnership of justice with love, sexual justice-love may not be a moral vision they can easily recognize or claim as Christian. There are real and very serious divisions on these matters. Conflict runs deep. People who are relatively well-protected and privileged often fail to hear the radicality of the gospel's call to rightly ordered community or the transformative power of its invitation to solidarity with outcasts. The gospel turns things upside down, subverts status quo expectations, and reverses roles so that the first become last, the poor rich, and the outsider is brought inside and given an honored place among co-equals.[3] A liberating Christianity takes delight in and affirms the incomparable worth of the *particular, concrete* spirits and bodies of women, gay/lesbian/bisexual people, survivors of sexual violence, and all other "culturally despised persons" of all colors. Granting an honored place to "unimportant" people is the pathway today, as it was in the early Jesus movement, for revitalizing the body and soul of community.

Reclaiming an Erotic Spirituality

Gay men, lesbian women, and bisexual people of faith, once hidden at the margins, are now insisting on visibility, claiming our rightful place alongside others, and carrying forward a distinctive moral vision. Our mission begins by making our presence known and our voices heard. We insist on being treated as all people should be—with dignity, compassion, and fairness. However, we are not just like others. Our perspectives, theologies, and moral vision are shaped differently by our social location as marginalized persons and by our resistance to injustice. Our commitments to a justice inclusive of our own dignity create a moral restlessness in us determined to resist dehumanization and degradation, no matter where these occur.

Our calling is to transform culture, including religious tradition, in the direction of a radically inclusive justice. Staying loyal to the Spirit of justice means putting our bodies on the line wherever there is a cry of injustice.

115

It means trusting, deep down, that God's creation, including our own body spirits, will not cease groaning until justice and love embrace throughout the cosmos.

The Radical Right warns endlessly about a subversive "gay agenda" but misses the point entirely that subverting social injustice is a noble calling. The struggle to undermine unjust, dehumanizing conditions that block personal and communal well-being is actually never-ending. Justice-committed gay, lesbian, and bisexual people must resist social oppression in all its varieties and must strengthen the bonds of genuine community. We must also stand up to those who say that our sin is that we flaunt our sexuality. Yes, there is little doubt that we provoke the dominant culture because we celebrate the spiritual energy that flows through the body and because we are not ashamed of our desire for loving, bodily embrace. We prize eroticism as a spiritual resource and speak about this openly. For this reason some seek to discredit us by accusing us of recruiting and endangering youth. On this score, perhaps we should candidly admit that the only kind of recruitment we are interested in is of an ethical, not a sexual, nature. We endanger the status quo by insisting on our self-respect and by building coalitions with nongay people in order to extend justice everywhere. We intentionally and unapologetically recruit persons of all colors, classes, and sexualities to live dangerously and pursue love fearlessly.

Spirituality, as a whole-body valuing of the sacred in our lives, enfolds human sexualities in intimate, sometimes unsettling ways.[4] Many gay people recognize, first, that sexuality is a means of grace. Grace happens in and through our body touching. As the fourteenth-century nun Dame Julian of Norwich affirmed, "our sensuality is grounded in nature, in compassion, and in grace. In our sensuality, God is." Second, we understand that a body-affirming, justice-centered spirituality must trust, despite all the evidence to the contrary, that "God's very being still becomes flesh and dwells among us full of grace and truth."[5] The power of the Sacred is en-fleshed or, as traditionally affirmed, encountered incarnationally. Where there is sensuous justice-love, God's power is known in and through that radical loving. When justice and compassion are extended, God becomes more firmly en-fleshed in our lives. Spiritually speaking, our calling is to *embrace more radically in our lives the enfleshing of the Sacred*.

There are, of course, conflicting Christian spiritualities. Two examples demonstrate the differences. The first shows the persistent influence of an otherworldly spirituality on Christian piety. Søren Kierkegaard, the nineteenth century Danish theologian, experienced an irreconcilable tension between human and divine love.[6] Kierkegaard had hoped to marry a young woman named Regina Olsen and earnestly pursued her even though she repeatedly turned down his marriage proposals. After she finally agreed to marry him, Kierkegaard broke off their engagement because of his fear that his love for a woman would jeopardize his ability to love God unreservedly. Dualistic, patriarchal Christianity taught him that devotion to God required denial of earthly delights. Insofar as love for another human being was a distraction from loving God, Kierkegaard resolved the tension by elevating love of God as superior to love of persons.

Kierkegaard's moral struggle is grounded in a dualistic theological worldview that diminishes human existence. The sacred is located outside people's lives, beyond human touch. Patriarchal spirituality ultimately fosters a quest for radical transcendence and total independence from others. Such a body-distancing spirituality encourages powerful men (and women who identify with patriarchal values) to seek absolute control. They imagine the good life as a life beyond vulnerability or intimate connection with others.

The moral problem generated by patriarchal spirituality is formidable. What is held sacred and worthy of loyalty is placed outside the realm of what is seen, heard, and touched. The sacred is projected well beyond people's bodies or their material connections with others. Such spiritual estrangement gives sanction for the abuse of bodies and the earth. By locating the sacred beyond the body, a patriarchal split consciousness allows people to inflict (and suffer) pain in pursuit of a wholly transcendent, nonmanifest good. Violence is rationalized in the name of defending abstractions, such as patriarchy's "lord god almighty," "Western civilization," and "a man's home is his castle." These abstractions turn people's attention away from the embodied, sensuous web of life that sustains and enlivens their living.

In contrast, a liberating commitment to justice-love images the good life in terms of honoring as sacred both our bodies and our flesh-and-blood connections. Justice-love, by insisting on the sanctity of every body, operates with a radically different notion of transcendence and the holy. In liberation perspective, transcendence is not a quest for control or mastery. Rather, transcendence is the capacity to turn more attentively toward the familiar and evident, to enjoy the pleasure of at-homeness in our bodies and communities, and to risk the vulnerability of being altered by our associations with others. This experience of the sacred, however partial and incomplete in our lives, affirms that gentleness can cohabit gracefully with power, making life joyful and worth living. Liberating faith celebrates the blessed ties that bind together all that is. This binding together makes solidarity imaginable—our belonging together at the root to others, including other earth creatures and this fragile planet. Spirituality that is genuinely liberating refuses to sever love of God from love of this world.

To split God-love from human loving, as Martin Buber explains, is sublimely to misunderstand God.

> Creation is not a hurdle on the road to God, it is the road itself. We are created along with one another and directed to a life with one another. Creatures are placed in my way so that I, their fellow-creature, by means of them and with them, find the way to God. A God reached by their exclusion would not be the God of all lives in whom all life is fulfilled. . . . God wants us to come to God by means of the Reginas [and the Rogers] God has created, and not by renunciation of them.[7]

A this-worldly spirituality honors the unity of human personhood as a spirit/body whole and celebrates the presence of divine love mediated through human relationships. Spirituality and sexuality are, as theologian Robert McAfee Brown writes, "intimately and inextricably bound together, two expressions of a single basic reality rather than two different realities."[8]

This alternative, body-affirming spirituality is depicted in Toni Morrison's novel *Beloved*. A holy woman, Baby Suggs, preaches a powerful message that nonnormative bodies, too, are inviolate, but their integrity is not secured without struggle and courageous self-assertion:

> [Baby Suggs] told them that the only grace they could have was the grace they could imagine. That if they could not see it, they would not have it.
> "Here," she said, "in this here place, we love flesh; flesh that weeps, laughs; flesh that dances on bare feet in grass. Love it. Love it hard. Yonder they do not love your flesh. They despise it. . . . *You* got to love it. This is flesh I'm talking about here. Flesh that needs to be loved. . . . Love your neck; put a hand on it, grace it, stroke it and hold it up."[9]

As exemplified here, a this-worldly erotic spirituality would never envision salvation as escape from the body or as a turning away from the embodied goodness surrounding us. The material, the mundane, and the corporeal are a primary locus for disclosure of human and divine power. Physical touch—"put a hand on it, grace it, stroke it and hold it up"—is a privileged mode of moral relating, able to communicate deep caring, mutual pleasure, and resistance to evil.

At its best the Christian moral life is about sharing power. Empowerment means aligning ourselves with that sacred power flowing through breasts, penises, clitorises, naked skin, tongues, fingers, and sweaty, quivering flesh. That power piques people's desire for wholeness, integrity, and at-one-ness with others and the created order. Sexuality and spirituality are unavoidably intertwined as life-giving desire for sensuous connection and radical communion. Sexual passion entices us to become vulnerable and to open ourselves to affirmation and care. Erotic desire energizes and keeps us in touch with that awesome power that moves our hearts and yet also, magnificently, turns the galaxies and rotates the stars above.

An incarnational faith skittish about eroticism and fearful of body pleasure may well bore itself to death, but I doubt that patriarchal Christianity will have such a peaceful demise. If religious communities are to reclaim spiritual integrity, they must henceforth stop discouraging sensuous touch between consenting adults. The hate-filled trashing of gay/lesbian/bisexual people must cease. Women's power, including procreative power, must be affirmed and actively promoted as a community good. Real equality must be exhibited around race and class differences. If we are to attain some measure of sanity and maintain mutual respect for everyone, then we must redirect attention toward things that matter: toward encouraging responsible, loving relationships wherever they occur among the married and the single, among gays and lesbians, among young and old. Conventional categories—is it heterosexual? marital? monogamous? procreative?—no longer work in differentiating acceptable sexuality from unacceptable. These inherited categories distort rather than disclose what is most valuable about our relating. What matters ethically is the moral character and quality of our relationships. Not *who* we are, but *how* we are with each other is ethically significant. As James B. Nelson concludes, "Many religious people still learn to fear, despise, trivialize, and be ashamed of their bodies. But if we do not know the good news of God in our bodies, we may never know it."[10]

Getting Passionate about Justice

Gay men, lesbian women, and bisexual persons of all colors sustain hope for radical change in church and society by fervently holding onto the conviction that God-knowing and justice-making are intimately bound together. God's life-giving presence is known in our doing justice together, in preserving and enhancing the integrity of creation. Any community that fails to correct harmful power relations between individuals and groups is functionally atheistic, no matter what is professed publicly. Our human vocation finds its wellspring in God's sacred power that, against all odds, builds community where there is no community, strengthens right-relatedness among strangers and enemies, and welcomes persons home to their bodies and to the corporate, shared body. Celebrating body connectedness, reveling in a deep passion for life, and constructing a liveable future for this fragile planet are religiously mean-ingful ways to honor the body as the spirit's homeplace. Reverence for the body and delight in communal solidarity are the two marks of a genuinely liberating spirituality.

A justice-centered faith inspires us to become bolder, more coura-geous, and more spirited dissidents of the prevailing cultural dis-order. Gay, lesbian, and bisexual people, as well as our allies, could easily be intimidated by the forces arrayed against us, but we have made an amaz-ing discovery. We have learned in our struggles for visibility and survival that the source of our spiritual vitality is the *godly power of loving body touch*. Such loving includes a justice-loving commitment to make com-munities more inclusive and welcoming of diversity. Through body work, both personally and politically, we are discovering our spiritual strength.

The subversive moral knowledge that gay, lesbian, and bisexual per-sons carry in this culture is that transformative power lies in making body connections. Our power lies in sustaining erotic connections sparked by mutual respect, desire, and compassion. Strong, morally principled eroti-cism gladdens people's hearts, minds, and souls, as well as their bodies. Despite the cultural pressure to denigrate the body and render body loving shameful, we refuse to disembody love by spiritualizing it as a supposedly "higher," reputedly "more Christian" love, untainted by human desire. From a countercultural perspective, the love we need is grounded in jus-tice as mutual respect. This body-grounded love refuses to put up with abuse, injustice, or mean-spiritedness. Body-to-body love releases spiritual power. Without minimizing the risks involved in sharing vulnerabilities across the borders of our different skins, we can revel in the fact that sen-suous touch fortifies us to resist whatever devalues and renders us invisi-ble. In our sensuality we find moral strength. This is a moral strength born of God, a strength to say "no" to injustice and to say an equally resounding "yes" to whatever promotes life, dignity, and hope throughout creation.

Gay, lesbian, and bisexual people have had few resources for protect-ing our human rights, defending our homes and loved ones against vio-lence, or warding off debilitating hate campaigns. Miraculously, we have had one notable power, our lovemaking, to sustain our spirits. Our loving sensuality has kept us in touch with life's goodness despite present ills or our uncertainty about the future. Against the radical body hate in this cul-ture, we communicate a radical, life-giving message: Bodies are holy ground, sacred and inviolate. *They* are sacred. *We* are sacred. Grace in our lives is grace in and through our bodies.

The moral wisdom of gay people challenges other liberation theolo-gies. Every spirituality aimed at liberation focuses on a particular threat to a people and their struggle to rebuild community. An erotic spirituality of body justice moves beyond a single-minded focus on struggle. Gay/lesbian/bisexual spirituality is also, and perhaps even primarily, a *spirituality of earthly delight*, encouraging enjoyment of everyday life. It invites people to pay closer attention to what feels right, true, and good in their lives.[11] Gay, lesbian, and bisexual people know great suffering, but we also know the redemptive value of playing, giving parties, and celebrating. We are firmly persuaded that salvation, the communal experience of well-being, happens through our sensuous, imperfect, yet remarkably wonderful bodies, or it does not happen in any way truly believable for us.

As one among other people "disposed of" by patriarchal religious traditions, we may be tempted to reject spirituality entirely. For some, that move may be strategically necessary to ensure survival and therefore should be supported. It should also be recognized as a critique of conventional Christianity, which has been the cause of great pain and violence for many marginalized peoples. Another option, however, is to choose with care among conflicting spiritualities and become architects of a liberating spirituality that will truly honor us and all other persons. The wager some of us are willing to make is that the most authentic expression of Christianity, in keeping with its core values, is a Christianity that is actively antiracist, antisexist, and antihomophobic.[12] The risk we run by rejecting spirituality entirely is that we may lose a dimension of depth and empowerment that adds sparkle, imagination, and energy to our joys and struggles.

An erotic spirituality empowers us to stand together and trust, deep down, that we deserve a blessing, not a curse. The same blessing awaits all creation. This blessing will not be forthcoming, however, without liberating, justice-loving faith communities that are at home on the margins and able to construct what bell hooks calls "space[s] of radical openness."[13] This kind of marginality is not, as she explains, "a marginality one wishes to lose—to give up or surrender as part of moving into the center—but rather a site one stays in, clings to even, because it nourishes one's capacity to resist."[14] Gay, lesbian, and bisexual people need church in this sense. We need communities of spirited resistance, offering relatively safe and secure places to dream dreams of a world without homophobia, racism, sexism, and other oppressions.[15] We need nurturing places to protest against routinized brutalization and moral indifference, to celebrate our survival, and to keep us receptive to justice claims from beyond ourselves.

Emancipatory communities serve as training sites for radical loving and solidarity across socially constructed differences. As ethicist Larry Rasmussen explains, "Even irrepressible dreamers know that nothing is ever real until it is embodied, however. What counts with God and one another is not 'opportunity,' or even vision, but incarnation." Therefore, "What carries power and promise and generates conviction and courage is concrete community."[16] I agree wholeheartedly. A truly liberating spirituality is sustained by those multicultural, richly diverse communities where people are deeply respected and where their hunger and thirst for righteousness, justice, and joy are encouraged to increase.

In a time of profound cultural crisis, justice-loving people everywhere struggle to gain their moral bearings and to plot a liberating course. As they and we struggle to embody personal integrity and promote communal well-being, we find ourselves standing in a unique position to discover something rather remarkable: Embracing the body and pursuing erotic justice is an unexpected yet delightful pathway for spiritual renewal and replenishment. Nevertheless, the moral, spiritual, and political transformations most needed at this time cannot be manufactured by any one person or group simply at will. It is true that careful discernment can sometimes anticipate the arrival of transformative moments. At other times, what theologian Dorothee Soelle calls our "revolutionary patience"[17] may even hurry these transformations along. Our embodied passion for justice-love makes a difference even though the difference may be less than we hoped for.

Surging passions in body and spirit continue to make us restless. Our peace is disturbed, and therein lies hope. Impatience with injustice is a mighty force, and it can move us to transform our lives and remake the world. We passionately yearn for a radically different family, workplace, church, and society where we can be met and valued as persons of incomparable value. We are tantalized by visions of more respectful, caring, and pleasurable ways to live in our bodies and in the company of others.

These restless, unsettling passions run through us, making us toss and turn, all a sure sign that God is doing a new thing in our midst. In our passion for justice-love, we discover that we are never alone. God, the sacred Source of erotic delight, abides with us and awaits our decision to take a wild, liberating plunge, together, into ecstacy. This invitation is extended to us as a gift and as a task. What are we waiting for?

Notes

Notes to Introduction.
Needed: Liberating Moral Discourse on Sexuality

1. Larry J. Uhrig, *Sex Positive: A Gay Contribution to Sexual and Spiritual Union* (Boston: Alyson Publications, 1986), 9.
2. James B. Nelson, "Needed: A Continuing Sexual Revolution," in *Sexual Ethics and the Church: After the Revolution* (Chicago: Christian Century Foundation, 1989), 63–64.
3. Loren B. Mead, *The Once and Future Church: Reinventing the Congregation for a New Mission Frontier* (New York: Alban Institute, 1991), and also his *Transforming Congregations for the Future* (New York: Alban Institute, 1994), esp. chap. 1, "The Storm We Are In: It's Worse Than We Thought," 1–23.
4. Geneva Overholser, "The Last Bastion of Denial," *Des Moines Register*, 30 June 1991.
5. Daniel C. Maguire, *The Moral Core of Judaism and Christianity: Reclaiming the Revolution* (Minneapolis: Fortress Press, 1993).
6. Daniel C. Maguire, "The Feminization of God and Ethics," in *The Moral Revolution: A Christian Humanist Vision* (San Francisco: Harper & Row, 1986), 105–121.
7. Beverly Harrison argues that mutual love is "love in its deepest radicality" and that "the power of love [is] the real pleasure of mutual vulnerability, the experience of truly being cared for or of actively caring for another," in Beverly Wildung Harrison, *Making the Connections: Essays in Feminist Ethics*, ed. Carol S. Robb (Boston: Beacon Press, 1985), 18. See also Christine E. Gudorf, "Parenting, Mutual Love, and Sacrifice," in *Women's Consciousness, Women's Conscience: A Reader in Feminist Ethics*, ed. Barbara Hilkert Andolsen, Christine E. Gudorf, and Mary D. Pellauer (New York: Winston Press, 1985), 175–91.
8. Bernard Loomer, "Two Conceptions of Power," *Criterion* 15, no. 1 (winter 1976): 12–29. Loomer describes control or unilateral power as alienating power, the continual use of which "breeds an insensitivity to the presence of the other—again, whether the other be a person or nature or God" (18). The alternative is mutual or relational power, which Loomer defines as "the ability both to produce and to undergo an effect. It is the capacity both to influence others and to be influenced by others" (20). Such relational power is not weak, but in fact powerful: "Our readiness to take account of the feelings and values of another is a way of including the other within our world of meaning

and concern. At its best, receiving is not unresponsive passivity; it is an active openness. Our reception of another indicates that we are or may become large enough to make room for another within ourselves. . . . The strength of our security may well mean that we do not fear the other, that the other is not an overpowering threat to our own sense of worth" (21).

9. On women's struggles to leave abusive situations, see Ginny NiCarthy, *Getting Free: You Can End Abuse and Take Back Your Life* (Seattle, Wash.: Seal Press, 1982); Susan Schechter, *Women and Male Violence: The Visions and Struggles of the Battered Women's Movement* (Boston: South End Press, 1982); R. Emerson Dobash and Russell Dobash, *Violence against Wives: A Case against the Patriarchy* (New York: Free Press, 1979); and Joy M. K. Bussert, *Battered Women: From a Theology of Suffering to an Ethic of Empowerment* (New York: Division for Mission in North America, Lutheran Church in America, 1986).

10. Susan Moller Okin, *Justice, Gender, and the Family* (New York: Basic Books, 1989), 15, 22 (emphasis in original).

11. Barbara H. Andolsen, "Whose Sexuality? Whose Tradition? Women, Experience, and Roman Catholic Sexual Ethics," in *Religion and Sexual Health: Ethical, Theological, and Clinical Perspectives*, ed. Ronald M. Green (Boston: Kluwer Academic Publishers, 1992), 57.

12. Iris Young, *Justice and the Politics of Difference* (Princeton: Princeton University Press, 1990), 4.

13. Suzanne C. Toten, "The Methodology of Liberation Theology," in *World Hunger: The Responsibility of Christian Education* (Maryknoll, N.Y.: Orbis Books, 1982), 91–93.

14. Walter Brueggemann, "Voices of the Night—Against Justice," in Walter Brueggemann, Sharon Parks, and Thomas H. Groome, *To Act Justly, Love Tenderly, Walk Humbly: An Agenda for Ministers* (New York: Paulist Press, 1986), 15.

15. This phrase first appears in the Presbyterian study document produced by the General Assembly Special Committee on Human Sexuality, Presbyterian Church (U.S.A.), *Keeping Body and Soul Together: Sexuality, Spirituality, and Social Justice* (Louisville, Ky.: Office of the General Assembly, 1991), 18, passim: "To do justice-love means seeking right-relatedness with others and working to set right all wrong relations, especially distorted power dynamics of domination and subordination." Christian ethicist Karen Lebacqz, in reviewing the study document, commented that justice-love and right-relation are rather awkward phrases, but are "meant to convey the notion that God demands nothing more nor less than justice and love intertwined, and that *any* human activity that does not exhibit both love and justice is wrong." Karen Lebacqz, "Sex: Justice in Church and Society," *Christianity and Crisis* (27 May 1991): 174.

Notes to Chapter 1.
Rethinking Sexuality

1. Carter Heyward, *Touching Our Strength: The Erotic as Power and the Love of God* (San Francisco: Harper & Row, 1989), 4.
2. The General Assembly Special Committee on Human Sexuality, Presbyterian Church (U.S.A.), "Keeping Body and Soul Together: Sexuality, Spirituality, and Social Justice" (Louisville, Ky.: Office of the General Assembly, Presbyterian Church [U.S.A.], 1991), 6. This report was reprinted as *Presbyterians and Human Sexuality 1991* (Louisville, Ky.: Office of the General Assembly, Presbyterian Church [U.S.A.], 1991).
3. Margaret A. Farley, "An Ethic for Same-Sex Relations," in *A Challenge to Love: Gay and Lesbian Catholics in the Church*, ed. Robert Nugent (New York: Crossroad, 1986), 93.
4. Mary Douglas, *Purity and Danger: An Analysis of Concepts of Pollution and Taboo* (London: Routledge & Kegan Paul, 1966), 122, 3f. Cited in James B. Nelson, *Embodiment: An Approach to Sexuality and Christian Theology* (Minneapolis: Augsburg Publishing House, 1978), 22.
5. Jeffrey Weeks, *Sexuality* (New York: Tavistock Publications, 1986), 106.
6. For a historical perspective on sexuality in the United States and on the patterning of erotic life, see John D'Emilio and Estelle B. Freedman, *Intimate Matters: A History of Sexuality in America* (New York: Harper & Row, 1988).
7. Karen L. Bloomquist, "The Politics of Sex and Power in the Churches" (n. p., 1 March 1993): 2.
8. James Davison Hunter, *Culture Wars: The Struggle to Define America* (New York: Basic Books, 1991), 52.
9. Gayle S. Rubin, "Thinking Sex: Notes for a Radical Theory of the Politics of Sexuality," in *The Lesbian and Gay Studies Reader*, ed. Henry Abelove, Michele Aina Barale, and David M. Halperin (New York: Routledge & Kegan Paul, 1993), 3-4.
10. Womanist theologian Delores Williams recommends these two criteria, survival and quality of life, for moral evaluation in her *Sisters in the Wilderness: The Challenge of Womanist God-Talk* (Maryknoll, N.Y.: Orbis Books, 1993), esp. 170-77.
11. See "The Rise and Fall of Sexual Liberalism, 1920 to the Present," in John D'Emilio and Estelle B. Freedman, *Intimate Matters: A History of Sexuality in America* (New York: Harper & Row, 1988), 239-360. Also Jeffrey Weeks, *Sexuality and Its Discontents: Meanings, Myths, and Modern Sexualities* (London: Routledge & Kegan Paul, 1985).
12. Mariana Valverde, *Sex, Power and Pleasure* (Toronto: Women's Press, 1985), 153.
13. Rubin, "Thinking Sex," 14-15.
14. William Sloane Coffin, *A Passion for the Possible: A Message to U.S. Churches* (Louisville, Ky.: Westminster/John Knox Press, 1993), 59.

15. See Susan Schechter, *Women and Male Violence* (Boston: South End Press, 1982); Joy M. K. Bussert, *Battered Women: From a Theology of Suffering to an Ethic of Empowerment* (New York: Lutheran Church in America, 1986); and Marie Marshall Fortune, *Sexual Violence: The Unmentionable Sin* (New York: Pilgrim Press, 1983); Carol J. Adams, *Woman-Battering* (Minneapolis: Fortress Press, 1994); and Joanne Carlson Brown and Carle R. Bohn, eds., *Christianity, Patriarchy, and Abuse: A Feminist Critique* (New York: Pilgrim Press, 1989).
16. Elizabeth Janeway, *Powers of the Weak* (New York: Morrow Quill Paperbacks, 1981), esp. chaps. 11 and 12, 157–85.
17. James B. Nelson, *Between Two Gardens: Reflections on Sexuality and Religious Experience* (New York: Pilgrim Press, 1983), 5–6.
18. James B. Nelson, *Embodiment: An Approach to Sexuality and Christian Theology* (Minneapolis: Augsburg Publishing House, 1978), 40.
19. Patricia Beattie Jung and Ralph F. Smith, *Heterosexism: An Ethical Challenge* (Albany, N.Y.: State University of New York Press, 1993).
20. Rubin, "Thinking Sex," 11.
21. Suzanne Pharr, *Homophobia: A Weapon of Sexism* (Inverness, Calif.: Chardon Press, 1988), 23.
22. Rubin, "Thinking Sex," 12.
23. Karen Lebacqz, *Justice in an Unjust World: Foundations for a Christian Approach to Justice* (Minneapolis: Augsburg Publishing House, 1987), 10.

Notes to Chapter 2.
Facing the Moral Problem

1. Sheila Briggs, "Sexual Justice and the 'Righteousness of God'," in *Sex and God: Some Varieties of Women's Religious Experience*, ed. Linda Hurcombe (New York: Routledge & Kegan Paul, 1987), 251.
2. Mariana Valverde, *Sex, Power and Pleasure* (Toronto: Women's Press, 1985), 14.
3. Jeffrey Weeks, *Sexuality* (New York: Tavistock Publications, 1986), 11.
4. Carter Heyward, *Touching Our Strength: The Erotic as Power and the Love of God* (San Francisco: Harper & Row, 1989), 50.
5. Robin Smith, *Living in Covenant with God and One Another* (Geneva: World Council of Churches Family Education Office, 1990), 167.
6. Gayle S. Rubin, "Thinking Sex: Notes for a Radical Theory of the Politics of Sexuality," in *The Lesbian and Gay Studies Reader*, ed. Henry Abelove, Michele Aina Barale, and David M. Halperin (New York: Routledge & Kegan Paul, 1993), 9.
7. Michael S. Kimmel, "Introduction: Guilty Pleasures—Pornography in Men's Lives," in *Men Confront Pornography*, ed. Michael S. Kimmel (New York: Crown Publishers, 1990), 4 (emphasis in original).
8. Ibid., 4–5.
9. Weeks, *Sexuality*, 24–25.

10. John D'Emilio and Estelle B. Freedman, *Intimate Matters: A History of Sexuality in America* (New York: Harper & Row, 1988).
11. Wilson Yates, "Human Sexuality: Dualistic and Holistic Paradigms," in Sylvia Thorson-Smith, *Pornography: Far From the Song of Songs* (Louisville, Ky.: Office of the General Assembly, Presbyterian Church [U.S.A.], 1988), 108.
12. Thomas Laqueur, *Making Sex: Body and Gender from the Greeks to Freud* (Cambridge, Mass.: Harvard University Press, 1990), viii, 4-6.
13. Ibid., 10, 21.
14. Ibid., 3-4.
15. Cited in "Introduction," *Homosexuality and Ethics*, ed. Edward Batchelor, Jr. (New York: Pilgrim Press, 1980), xvii.
16. For example, see Jeannine Gramick, "Prejudice, Religion, and Homosexual People," in *A Challenge to Love: Gay and Lesbian Catholics in the Church*, ed. Robert Nugent (New York: Crossroad, 1986), 3-19.
17. United Presbyterian Church in the U.S.A., *The Church and Homosexuality* (New York: Office of the General Assembly, 1978), D-23.
18. Boston Women's Health Book Collective, *The New Our Bodies/Ourselves: A Book By and For Women* (New York: Simon and Schuster, 1992). See also Ruth Bell et al., *Changing Bodies, Changing Lives: A Book for Teens on Sex and Relationships* (New York: Vintage Books, 1988), and Paula Brown Doress, Diana Laskin Siegal, and the Mid-Life and Older Women Book Project, *Ourselves, Growing Older: Women Aging with Knowledge and Power* (New York: Simon and Schuster, 1987).
19. Barbara Ehrenreich, Elizabeth Hess, and Gloria Jacobs, *Re-Making Love: The Feminization of Sex* (New York: Anchor Books, 1986), 5, 7.
20. James B. Nelson, *Embodiment: An Approach to Sexuality and Christian Theology* (Minneapolis: Augsburg Publishing House, 1978), 173. See also Donald Capps, "The Deadly Sins and Saving Virtues: How They Are Viewed by Clergy," *Pastoral Psychology* 40:4 (1992): 209-23.
21. Rosemary Radford Ruether, *Sexism and God-Talk: Toward a Feminist Theology* (Boston: Beacon Press, 1983), 183.
22. William Simon and John Gagnon, "Psychosexual Development," in *Human Sexuality: Contemporary Perspectives*, 2d ed., ed. Eleanor S. Morrison and Vera Borosage (Palo Alto, Calif.: Mayfield Publishing Co., 1977), 9-26. "We see sexual behavior therefore," they write, "as *scripted* behavior, not the masked expression of a primordial drive" (11). See also John H. Gagnon, *The Sexual Scene*, 2d ed. (New Brunswick, N.J.: Transaction Books, 1973).
23. Kimmel, "Guilty Pleasures," 7.
24. Beverly Wildung Harrison, *Making the Connections: Essays in Feminist Social Ethics*, ed. Carol S. Robb (Boston: Beacon Press, 1985), 149.
25. Irving Kenneth Zola, *Missing Pieces: A Chronicle of Living with a Disability* (Philadelphia: Temple University Press, 1982), 214. See also Debra Connors, "Disability, Sexism, and the Social Order," in *Redefining Sexual Ethics: A Sourcebook of Essays, Stories, and Poems*, ed. Susan E. Davies and Eleanor H. Haney (Cleveland: Pilgrim Press, 1991), 167-80.

26. Zola, 215.
27. Susan Wendell, "Toward a Feminist Theory of Disability," *Hypatia: A Journal of Feminist Philosophy* 4:2 (Summer 1989): 104, 112.
28. Ynestra King, "The Other Body: Reflections on Difference, Disability, and Identity Politics," *Ms.* 3:5 (March–April 1993): 73.
29. Wendell, "Toward a Feminist Theory of Disability," 116.
30. King, "The Other Body," 75.
31. Wendell, "Toward a Feminist Theory of Disability," 116.
32. Charlotte Bunch, *Passionate Politics: Essays 1968-1986; Feminist Theory in Action* (New York: St. Martin's Press, 1987), 150–51.
33. Patricia Hill Collins, *Black Feminist Thought: Knowledge, Consciousness, and the Politics of Empowerment* (New York: Routledge & Kegan Paul, 1991), 182, 196.
34. Harrison, *Making the Connections*, 148.
35. Audre Lorde, *Sister Outsider: Essays and Speeches* (Trumansburg, N.Y.: Crossing Press, 1984), 45.
36. Cornel West, *Race Matters* (Boston: Beacon Press, 1993), 83.
37. Delores S. Williams, *Sisters of the Wilderness* (Maryknoll, N.Y.: Orbis Books, 1993), 85.
38. West, *Race Matters*, 83, 85, 86.
39. Williams, *Sisters of the Wilderness*, 71.
40. D'Emilio and Freedman, *Intimate Matters*, 86.
41. Marie Marshall Fortune, *Sexual Violence: The Unmentionable Sin; An Ethical and Pastoral Perspective* (New York: Pilgrim Press, 1983), 90.
42. Ibid.
43. For a discussion of incarceration rates in relation to gender, race, and class in the United States, see Piers Beirne and James Messerschmidt, *Criminology*, 2d ed. (New York: Harcourt Brace, 1995), esp. chaps. 2 and 4.
44. Angela Y. Davis, *Violence Against Women and the Ongoing Challenge to Racism* (Latham, N.Y.: Kitchen Table: Women of Color Press, 1985), 6.
45. Barbara and John Ehrenreich, "The System Behind the Chaos," in *The Crisis in Health Care: The Ethical Issues*, ed. Nancy F. McKenzie (New York: Meridian Books, 1990), 59. See also "Study: Blacks with Heart Trouble Get Less Care." *Bangor Daily News* 105:60 (26 August 1991), 1–2. Two studies, based on records from Veterans Administration hospitals, conclude that among all age groups blacks are significantly more likely than whites to suffer and die from a heart attack. These reports leave unanswered the risk involved for women of all colors, an example of the invisibility of women and especially black women in racist patriarchy.
46. Ibid.
47. bell hooks, *Black Looks: Race and Representation* (Boston: South End Press, 1992), 7.
48. West, *Race Matters*, 85.
49. Ibid., 96.
50. Collins, *Black Feminist Thought*, 170.

51. Ibid., 174.
52. A Presbyterian study of pornography, *Far From the Song of Songs*, lists the following characteristics of a patriarchal cultural system: "(a) mystification of sex based on ignorance of human sexuality; (b) the association of sex with evil; (c) the use of sex as an instrument of power; (d) economic discrimination against women; (e) the acceptance of violence as natural and inevitable; (f) the commercialization of human needs; (g) widespread addiction to obsessive-compulsive behavior; and (h) unequal responsibility for human relationship." As this study documents, the burgeoning pornography industry in the United States displays sexuality as a dynamic of dominance and subordination. Good sex is depicted as sex requiring inequalities of power and status between a man and a woman. In this regard pornography expresses mainstream cultural values about sex though, granted, in exaggerated display. "Whatever else it may tell us," this report concludes, "pornography offers irrefutable evidence that this culture is patriarchal" (66). Sylvia Thorson Smith, *Pornography: Far from the Song of Songs* (Louisville, Ky.: Office of the General Assembly, Presbyterian Church [U.S.A.], 1988).
53. John Stoltenberg, *Refusing to Be a Man: Essay on Sex and Justice* (Portland, Ore.: Breitenbush Books, 1989), 61.
54. See Fortune, *Sexual Violence*, esp. chap. 2, "Confusing Sexual Activity and Sexual Violence," 14-41.
55. Karen Lebacqz, "Loving Your Enemy: Sex, Power, and Christian Ethics," *The Annual of the Society of Christian Ethics*, ed. D. M. Yeager (Washington, D.C.: Georgetown University Press, 1990), 3-23.
56. Stoltenberg, *Refusing to Be a Man*, 13.
57. Weeks, *Sexuality*, 13.
58. Stoltenberg, 14.
59. Patricia Hill Collins, *Black Feminist Thought*, 198.
60. Stoltenberg, 31, 33.
61. Diana Scully, *Understanding Sexual Violence: A Study of Convicted Rapists* (Boston: Unwin Hyman, 1990), 149-50.
62. Ibid., 7, 8.
63. Rosemary Radford Ruether, "Homophobia, Heterosexism, and Pastoral Practice," in *Sexuality and the Sacred: Sources for Theological Reflection*, ed. James B. Nelson and Sandra P. Longfellow (Louisville, Ky.: Westminster/John Knox Press, 1994).
64. Rosemary Radford Ruether, "Catholicism, Women, Body and Sexuality: A Response," in *Women, Religion and Sexuality: Studies on the Impact of Religious Teaching on Women*, ed. Jeanne Becher (Philadelphia: Trinity Press International, 1990), 226.
65. On the confusion of sexuality and violence, see Marie Marshall Fortune, *Sexual Violence: The Unmentionable Sin, An Ethical and Pastoral Perspective* (New York: Pilgrim Press, 1983), esp. 14-41. Also Karen Lebacqz, "Loving Your Enemy: Sex, Power, and Christian Ethics," *The*

1990 Annual of the Society of Christian Ethics, ed. D. M. Yeager (Washington, D. C.: Georgetown University Press, 1990), 3–23.

66. Karen L. Bloomquist, "The Politics of Sex and Power in the Churches," (n. p., 1 March 1993), 4.

67. Ibid.

68. William Sloane Coffin, *A Passion for the Possible: A Message to U.S. Churches* (Louisville, Ky.: Westminster/John Knox Press, 1993), 88.

69. In 1990 the Kinsey Institute, in conjunction with the Roper Organization, conducted face-to-face interviews with nearly 2,000 people in a statistically representative sample of U.S. adults. The scores on the 18-question exam indicate the lack of accurate sex information for most adults. Only 5 percent of the sample population received a grade of A, while 82 percent failed or received a D. *Network News: Eastern Maine AIDS Network* 1:3 (December 1990): 4, 6.

70. Larry J. Uhrig, *Sex Positive: A Gay Contribution to Sexual and Spiritual Union* (Boston: Alyson Publications, 1986), 14.

Notes to Chapter 3.
Locating Resources for a Liberating Ethic

1. John Fortunato, "The Last Committee on Sexuality (Ever)," *Christianity and Crisis* 51:22 (18 February 1991): 34.

2. Vern L. Bullough, "Christianity and Sexuality," in *Religion and Sexual Health: Ethical, Theological, and Clinical Perspectives*, ed. Ronald M. Green (Boston: Kluwer Academic Publishers, 1992), 3.

3. Carter Heyward, *Our Passion for Justice: Images of Power, Sexuality, and Liberation* (New York: Pilgrim Press, 1984), esp. ch. 10, "Coming Out: Journey Without Maps," 75–82.

4. Beverly Wildung Harrison, *Our Right to Choose: Toward a New Ethic of Abortion* (Boston: Beacon Press, 1983), 119.

5. *Women, Religion and Sexuality: Studies on the Impact of Religious Teaching on Women*, ed. Jeanne Becher (Philadelphia: Trinity Press International, 1990), esp. Rosemary Radford Ruether, "Catholicism, Women, Body and Sexuality: A Response," 221–32.

6. Daniel C. Maguire, "The Shadow Side of the Homosexuality Debate," in *Homosexuality in the Priesthood and the Religious Life* (New York: Crossroad, 1989), 38–39.

7. James B. Nelson, "Body Theology and Human Sexuality," in *Religion and Sexual Health*, ed. Ronald M. Green, 43–44.

8. Bruce C. Birch and Larry L. Rasmussen, *Bible and Ethics in the Christian Life*, rev. and exp. ed. (Minneapolis: Augsburg, 1989), 175.

9. Carter Heyward, *Touching Our Strength: The Erotic as Power and the Love of God* (San Francisco: Harper & Row, 1989), 74.

10. bell hooks, *Talking Back: Thinking Feminist, Thinking Black* (Boston: South End Press, 1989), 18.

11. Birch and Rasmussen, *Bible and Ethics in the Christian Life*, 96.
12. William R. Stayton, "Conflicts in Crisis: Effects of Religious Belief Systems on Sexual Health," in *Religion and Sexual Health*, ed. Ronald M. Green, 203.
13. For a critical analysis of sexology as a discipline shaped ideologically, see Jeffrey Weeks, *Sex, Politics, and Society: The Regulation of Sexuality Since 1800* (London: Longman, 1981), and his *Sexuality and Its Discontents: Meanings, Myths, and Modern Sexualities* (London: Routledge & Kegan Paul, 1985).
14. Morris L. Floyd, "Sexual Ethics: A Gay Male Perspective," *Open Hands* 4:3 (winter 1989): 11.
15. Farley, "Sexual Ethics," 1584. My emphasis.
16. Judith Plaskow, *Standing Again at Sinai: Judaism from a Feminist Perspective* (San Francisco: Harper & Row, 1990), vii, x.
17. Ibid., 1.
18. Peggy Way, "An Authority of Possibility for Women in the Church," in *Women's Liberation and the Church*, ed. Sarah Bentley Doely (New York: Association Press, 1970). See also Letty M. Russell, *Household of Freedom: Authority in Feminist Theology* (Philadelphia: Westminster Press, 1987), and also her *Church in the Round: Feminist Interpretation of the Church* (Louisville, Ky.: Westminster/John Knox Press, 1993.
19. Elisabeth Schüssler Fiorenza, *Bread Not Stone: The Challenge of Feminist Biblical Interpretation* (Boston: Beacon Press, 1984), xiii–xiv.
20. Gary David Comstock, *Gay Theology Without Apology* (Cleveland: Pilgrim Press, 1993), 11–12.
21. Walter Brueggemann, "Textuality in the Church," in *Tensions Between Citizenship and Discipleship*, ed. Nelle G. Slater (New York: Pilgrim Press, 1989), 57.
22. Dan Spencer, "Church at the Margins," in *Sexuality and the Sacred: Sources for Theological Reflection*, ed. James B. Nelson and Sandra P. Longfellow (Louisville, Ky.: Westminster/John Knox Press, 1994), 398.
23. bell hooks, *Yearning: Race, Gender, and Cultural Politics* (Boston: South End Press, 1990), 149, 150.
24. Fiorenza, *Bread Not Stone*, 15, 19–20.
25. Phyllis Trible, *God and the Rhetoric of Sexuality* (Philadelphia: Fortress Press, 1978), 161–62.
26. Comstock, *Gay Theology Without Apology*, 44–45.
27. Renita J. Weems, "Song of Songs," in *The Women's Bible Commentary*, ed. Carol A. Newsom and Sharon H. Ringe (Louisville, Ky.: Westminster/John Knox Press, 1992), 159, 160.
28. Ibid., 160.
29. John Dominic Crossan, *Jesus: A Revolutionary Biography* (San Francisco: HarperSanFrancisco, 1994), esp. ch. 3, "A Kingdom of Nuisances and Nobodies," 54–74. Also Marcus J. Borg, *Meeting Jesus Again for the First Time: The Historical Jesus and the Heart of Contemporary Faith* (San

Francisco: HarperSanFrancisco, 1994), esp. ch. 3, "Jesus, Compassion, and Politics," 46–68.

30. Elisabeth Schüssler Fiorenza, *In Memory of Her: A Feminist Reconstruction of Christian Origins* (New York: Crossroad, 1983), esp. "The Basileia Vision of Jesus as the Praxis of Inclusive Wholeness," 118–30.

Notes to Chapter 4.
Reimagining Good Sex

1. Mary Hunt, "Sexual Ethics: A Lesbian Perspective," *Open Hands* 4:3 (winter 1989): 10.
2. Beverly Wildung Harrison, *Making the Connections: Essays in Feminist Social Ethics*, ed. Carol S. Robb (Boston: Beacon Press, 1985), 148.
3. Christine E. Gudorf, *Body, Sex, and Pleasure: Reconstructing Christian Sexual Ethics* (Cleveland: Pilgrim Press, 1994), esp. ch. 5.
4. Rebecca Parker, "Making Love as a Means of Grace: Women's Reflections," *Open Hands* 3:3 (winter 1988): 9, 12.
5. Beverly Wildung Harrison, "Human Sexuality and Mutuality," in *Christian Feminism: Visions of a New Humanity*, ed. Judith L. Weidman (San Francisco: Harper & Row, 1984), 148, 147.
6. Harrison, *Making the Connections*, 13.
7. Valverde, *Sex, Power, and Pleasure*, 43.
8. Parker, "Making Love as a Means of Grace," 12.
9. Karen Lebacqz and Ronald G. Barton point out that feminist and gay liberation epistemologies validate the authenticity of moral insights deriving from inner knowledge, "feelings," "intuition," and "trusting one's own experience." Trusting feelings, they argue, may have a different meaning and validity depending on whether one is from an oppressed or dominant group. But they also insist that these new epistemologies are not a reversion to subjectivism: "It is not in fact a purely 'subjective' form of knowledge but is a conclusion based on experience and observation and open to the confirmation of other knowers" (166) or, again, "the use of the language of 'feelings' is often a shorthand summary for what are in fact judgments well grounded in data that can be communicated to others" (166–67). *Sex in the Parish* (Louisville, Ky.: Westminster/John Knox Press, 1991). Also see Mary Field Belenky et al., *Women's Ways of Knowing: The Development of Self, Voice, and Mind* (New York: Basic Books, 1986).
10. James Wm. McClendon, Jr., "Towards an Ethics of Delight," in *Ethics, Religion, and the Good Society: New Directions in a Pluralistic World,* ed. Joseph Runzo (Louisville, Ky.: Westminster/John Knox Press, 1992), 53–54.
11. Audre Lorde, "Uses of the Erotic: The Erotic as Power," *Sister Outsider: Essays and Speeches* (Trumansburg, N.Y.: Crossing Press, 1984), 53, 57, 58.
12. Heyward, *Our Passion for Justice*, 140.

13. John Stoltenberg, *Refusing to Be a Man: Essays on Sex and Justice* (Portland, Ore.: Breitenbush Books, 1989), 37.
14. Diana E. H. Russell in *Rape in Marriage* (New York: Collier Books, 1982) reports the findings of one survey that 14% of women who had ever been married had been raped by a husband or an ex-husband. Russell argues, "To the extent that this finding may be generalized to the population at large, it suggests that at least one woman out of every seven who has ever been married has been raped by a husband at least once, and sometimes many times over many years (2). On the accuracy and significance of statistics about rape and other violences against women, children, and some men, see Barbara Chester, "The Statistics about Sexual Violence," in *Sexual Assault and Abuse: A Handbook for Clergy and Religious Professionals,* ed. Mary D. Pellauer, Barbara Chester, and Jane Boyajian (San Francisco: Harper & Row, 1987), 10–16.
15. Karen Lebacqz, "Appropriate Vulnerability: A Sexual Ethics for Singles," in *Sexual Ethics and the Church: A Christian Century Symposium* (Chicago: The Christian Century Foundation, 1989), 18–23.
16. James B. Nelson, *Between Two Gardens: Reflections on Sexuality and Religious Experience* (New York: Pilgrim Press, 1983), esp. chap. 6, "Singleness and the Church," 96–109.
17. Mary E. Hobgood, "Marriage, Market Values, and Social Justice: Toward an Examination of Compulsory Monogamy," in *Redefining Sexual Ethics: A Sourcebook of Essays, Stories, and Poems,* ed. Susan E. Davies and Eleanor H. Haney (Cleveland: Pilgrim Press, 1991), 116.
18. Ibid., 125.
19. L. William Countryman, *Dirt, Greed, and Sex: Sexual Ethics in the New Testament and Their Implications for Today* (Philadelphia: Fortress Press, 1988), 263.

Notes to Chapter 5.
Securing the Sanctity of Every Body

1. John Stoltenberg, "A coupla things I've been meaning to say about really confronting male power," *Changing Men* 22 (winter/spring 1991): 9.
2. On the confusion of sexuality and violence, see Marie Marshall Fortune, *Sexual Violence: The Unmentionable Sin* (New York: Pilgrim Press, 1983), 14–41; Carol Vance, ed., *Pleasure and Danger: Exploring Female Sexuality* (Boston: Routledge & Kegan Paul, 1985); and Beverly W. Harrison and Carter Heyward, "Pain and Pleasure: Avoiding the Confusions of Christian Tradition in Feminist Theory," in *Christianity, Patriarchy, and Abuse: A Feminist Critique,* ed. Joanne Carlson Brown and Carole R. Bohn (New York: Pilgrim Press, 1989), 148–73.
3. Survivors of intimate violence have an epistemological advantage in analyzing the ideological underpinnings of sexual and domestic violence and disclosing how cultural norms, including religious ones, have masked the

problem of male abuse of power. For an educational strategy that invites concrete answerability to victims/survivors in the development of theological claims, see Marvin M. Ellison and Kristina B. Hewey, "Hope Lies in 'The Struggle Against It': Co-Teaching a Seminary Course on Domestic Violence and Theology," in *Violence Against Women and Children: A Religious Sourcebook*, ed. Marie M. Fortune and Carol Adams (New York: Continuum, 1995), 504–43.

4. See "Myths and Facts about Sexual Assault and Child Sexual Abuse," and Barbara Chester, "The Statistics about Sexual Violence," in *Sexual Assault and Abuse: A Handbook for Clergy and Religious Professionals*, ed. Mary D. Pellauer, Barbara Chester, and Jane Boyajian (San Francisco: Harper & Row, 1987), 5–16.

5. Piers Beirne and James Messerschmidt, *Criminology*, 2d ed. (New York: Harcourt Brace, 1995), 140, 121.

6. Ibid., 125. Beirne and Messerschmidt also discuss prevalence rates. Wife battering occurs in approximately one-quarter to one-third of heterosexual couples. Most battered women, however, do not report their male partner's abuse. Researchers estimate that "approximately one in every 10 cases is reported to the police" (127).

7. Diana E. H. Russell, *Rape in Marriage* (New York: Collier Books, 1982), 64, 57.

8. Beirne and Messerschmidt, 124.

9. Gloria Steinem, "Foreword," in *Women Respond to the Men's Movement: A Feminist Collection*, ed. Kay Leigh Hagen (San Francisco: HarperSanFrancisco, 1992), vi.

10. This data is summarized by Mary D. Pellauer, "Moral Callousness and Moral Sensitivity: Violence Against Women," in Barbara Hilkert Andolsen, Christine E. Gudorf, and Mary D. Pellauer, *Women's Consciousness, Women's Conscience: A Reader in Feminist Ethics* (New York: Winston Press, 1985), 37–41. Beirne and Messerschmidt have reviewed studies of some 5,000 U.S. women, and from that data conclude that "from one-fifth to one-third of the women reported having had some sort of childhood sexual encounter with an adult male" (op. cit., 134).

11. Joy M. K. Bussert, *Battered Women: From a Theology of Suffering to an Ethic of Empowerment* (Lutheran Church in America: Division for Mission in North America, 1986), 23–24. About women who batter in lesbian relationships, see Barbara Hart, "Lesbian Battering: An Examination," in *Naming the Violence: Speaking Out About Lesbian Battering*, ed. Kerry Lobel (Seattle: Seal Press, 1986), 173–89. Hart's analysis is useful in assessing reasons some lesbians batter, reasons which are similar to those of male batterers: to gain victim compliance, because violence is often an effective method to achieve control over an intimate, and because using violence is relatively safe for the batterer, who believes (s)he will rarely face negative consequences. Lesbian battering, however, is distinguishable from male battering in at least three ways: (1) lesbians who are bat-

tered are typically even more reluctant than nonlesbians to go public about their violent partners; (2) the battered woman in a lesbian context may use physical means to resist and fight back more often than nonlesbians; and (3) astute listening and judgment skills are needed to correctly identify victim and victimizer since both women may speak of themselves as victimized.

12. For sociological and ethical-theological analysis of antigay violence, see Gary David Comstock, *Violence Against Lesbians and Gay Men* (New York: Columbia University Press, 1991).

13. Beirne and Messerschmidt, 139. My italics.

14. The picture changes somewhat when violence against children is introduced. Child sexual abuse is conducted primarily by adult heterosexual males against female children. However, "[adult] men and women each commit 50 percent of the physical abuse and neglect of children" (Beirne and Messerschmidt, 140).

15. Starhawk, "A Men's Movement I Can Trust," in *Women Respond to the Men's Movement*, ed. Kay Leigh Hagen, 34-35.

16. For a differentiation among men's movements, see James B. Nelson, *Body Theology* (Louisville, Ky.: Westminster/John Knox Press, 1992), 76-80. Also John J. Carey, "A Christian Ethicist Looks at the Men's Movement," (Agnes Scott College, n.d.). For an insightful, profeminist analysis of various theoretical approaches to counseling male batterers, see David Adams, "Treatment Models of Men Who Batter: A Profeminist Analysis," in *Feminist Perspectives on Wife Abuse*, ed. Kersti Yllö and Michele Bograd (Newbury Park: Sage Publications, 1990), 176-99.

17. Steinem, in Hagen, vii.

18. Starhawk, in Hagen, 28.

19. Susan Schechter, *Women and Male Violence: The Visions and Struggles of the Battered Women's Movement* (Boston: South End Press, 1982), 238.

20. Rosemary Radford Ruether, *Sexism and God-Talk: Toward a Feminist Theology* (Boston: Beacon Press, 1983), 178.

21. Bernard Loomer differentiates between unilateral and relational power in his "Two Conceptions of Power," *Criterion* 15:1 (winter 1976): 12-29. Relational power, which I am calling moral power, is the capacity to sustain a mutual relationship. Mutuality signals the shared process of "making claims and permitting and enabling others to make their claims" (23). Men who batter refuse to acknowledge their victim's right to make reciprocal claims on them. Loomer also argues that "the world of the individual who can be influenced by another without losing his or her identity or freedom is larger than the world of the individual who fears being influenced" (21). For a feminist analysis that draws on Loomer's work, see Rita Nakashima Brock, *Journeys by Heart: A Christology of Erotic Power* (New York: Crossroad, 1988).

22. On the question of "appropriate" victim, see R. Emerson Dobash and Russell Dobash, *Violence Against Wives: A Case Against the Patriarchy*

(New York: Free Press, 1979), esp. ch. 3, "The Legacy of the 'Appropriate' Victim," 31–47.

23. Suzanne Pharr, *Homophobia: A Weapon of Sexism* (Inverness, Calif.: Chardon Press, 1988), esp. 1–26.

24. Mariana Valverde, *Sex, Power, and Pleasure* (Toronto: Women's Press, 1985), 19.

25. Beverly Wildung Harrison, *Making the Connections: Essays in Feminist Social Ethics*, ed. Carol S. Robb (Boston: Beacon Press, 1985), 233–34.

26. Wayne Eisenhart, USMC, quoted by Rick Ritter, "Bringing War Home: Vets Who Have Battered," in *Battered Women's Directory*, 9th ed., ed. Betsy Warrior (Richmond, Ind.: Earlham College, 1985), 254.

27. Richard Goldstein, "The Coming Crisis of Gay Rights," in *The Village Voice* 39:26 (28 June 1994): 25–29. Goldstein argues that "the most important alliance we can make is the bond between queers and feminists," and further, that "our struggle must be not to build a queer nation, but a world where both sexes have an equal impact on the formation of values" (28).

28. J. Glenn Gray, *The Warriors: Reflections on Men in Battle* (New York: Harper & Row, 1970), xviii.

29. Diana Scully, *Understanding Sexual Violence: A Study of Convicted Rapists* (Boston: Unwin Hyman, 1990), 106.

30. Gray, *The Warriors*, esp. 167–69 and 215–42.

31. Joseph H. Pleck, "Men's Power with Women, Other Men, and Society: A Men's Movement Analysis," in *The American Man*, ed. Elizabeth H. Pleck and Joseph H. Pleck (Englewood Cliffs, N.J.: Prentice-Hall, 1980), 428.

32. For a narrative account of the destructiveness of internalized homophobia, see Paul Monette, *Becoming a Man: Half a Life Story* (New York: Harcourt Brace Jovanovich, 1992), an extended coming-out story about the struggles of claiming one's authenticity as male and gay in a culture that equates loving men with female desire, not male. For historical perspective, see George Chauncey's *Gay New York: Gender, Urban Culture, and the Making of the Gay Male World, 1890–1940* (New York: Basic Books, 1994). In working-class gay male culture prior to World War II, a distinction was commonly made between men who took the "active" role in anal/genital sex with other men (the inserters) and the "passive" partners (the insertees). The active male identified himself *as a man* and claimed that his masculinity was not called into question by his sexual activity. That was not the case for the receptive partner, often referred to as a "fairy" (neither male nor female) who became feminized because of his sexual role. Here, one's role as sexual dominant or subordinate, rather than sexual orientation or erotic preference, defined a person's gender identity. For the connections between homophobia and misogyny, see Harrison, *Making the Connections*, 135–51.

33. Audre Lorde, "Uses of the Erotic: The Erotic as Power," in *Take Back the Night: Women on Pornography*, ed. Laura Lederer (New York: William Morrow & Co., 1980), 299.

34. Carter Heyward, *Touching Our Strength: The Erotic as Power and the Love of God* (San Francisco: Harper & Row, 1989); Mary E. Hunt, *A Fierce Tenderness: Toward a Feminist Theology of Friendship* (San Francisco: Harper & Row, 1990); and Audre Lorde, "Uses of the Erotic: The Erotic as Power," in *Sister Outsider: Essays and Speeches* (Trumansburg, N.Y.: Crossing Press, 1984), 53–59.

35. Nelson, *The Intimate Connection*, 80.

36. Peggy Reeves Sanday, "The Socio-Cultural Context of Rape: A Cross-Cultural Study," *Journal of Social Issues* 37:4 (1981): 19.

37. Tony Eardley, "Violence and Sexuality," in *The Sexuality of Men*, ed. Andy Metcalf and Martin Humphries (London: Pluto Press, 1985), 86.

38. Gray, *The Warriors*, 175.

39. John Sabini and Maury Silver, *Moralities of Everyday Life* (New York: Oxford University Press, 1982), 83, 51.

40. On male entitlement to chastise and discipline women, see Bussert, *Battered Women*, 12–15.

41. For some feminist women's perspectives on male conversion and trustworthiness, see Rosemary Radford Ruether, *Sexism and God-Talk: Toward a Feminist Theology* (Boston: Beacon Press, 1983), 189–92; and Starhawk, "A Men's Movement I Can Trust," in Hagen, *Women Respond to the Men's Movement*, 27–37.

42. Barbara Smith, "Between a Rock and a Hard Place: Relationships Between Black and Jewish Women," in *Yours in Struggle: Three Feminist Perspectives on Anti-Semitism and Racism*, ed. Elly Bulkin, Minnie Bruce Pratt, and Barbara Smith (Brooklyn: Long Haul Press, 1984), 71.

43. John Stoltenberg, "A coupla things I've been meaning to say about really confronting male power," *Changing Men* 22 (winter–spring, 1991): 8.

44. Ibid., 9.

45. Charlotte Bunch, *Passionate Politics: Feminist Theory in Action* (New York: St. Martin's Press, 1987), 154.

46. Rosemary Radford Ruether, "Patriarchy and the Men's Movement: Part of the Problem or Part of the Solution?," in Hagen, *Women Respond to the Men's Movement*, 17.

47. Michael Biernbaum and Joseph Weinberg, "Men Unlearning Rape," *Changing Men* 22 (winter–spring 1991): 23.

Notes to Conclusion.
Reveling in an Erotic Spirituality of Justice

1. Melanie Kaye/Kantrowitz, *The Issue Is Power: Essays on Women, Jews, Violence and Resistance* (San Francisco: Aunt Lute Books, 1992), 90.

2. See Introduction, n. 15.

3. Historian John Boswell makes a helpful distinction among three distinct social categories: distinguishable insider, inferior insider, and outsider, in "Homosexuality and Religious Life: A Historical Approach," in *Sexuality*

and the Sacred: Sources for Theological Reflection, ed. James B. Nelson
and Sandra P. Longfellow (Louisville, Ky.: Westminster/John Knox Press,
1994), 361.

4. Nelson and Longfellow, *Sexuality and the Sacred*, xiv.

5. Ibid.

6. For this discussion I am indebted to Robert McAfee Brown, "A Case Study:
Spirituality and Sexuality," in *Spirituality and Liberation: Overcoming
the Great Fallacy* (Philadelphia: Westminster Press, 1988), 97-108.

7. Martin Buber, *Between Man and Man* (New York: Macmillan Co., 1965),
52, quoted in Brown, *Spirituality and Liberation*, 104-5.

8. Brown, 100.

9. Toni Morrison, *Beloved: A Novel* (New York: Alfred A. Knopf, 1987), 88.

10. James B. Nelson, "A Statement for the Sexuality Task Force: Presbyterian
Church USA, July 1, 1989," (n.p., n.d.), 10.

11. Audre Lorde, "Uses of the Erotic: The Erotic as Power," in *Sexuality and
the Sacred*, ed. Nelson and Longfellow, 75-79. Lorde suggests that the
erotic as our capacity for joy can be "the nursemaid of all our deepest
knowledge" and a lens "through which we scrutinize all aspects of our
existence" and judge how "not to settle for the convenient, the shoddy,
the conventionally expected, nor the merely safe" (77-78). See also
Beverly Wildung Harrison, *Making the Connection: Essays in Feminist
Social Ethics*, ed. Carol S. Robb (Boston: Beacon Press, 1984), esp. "The
Power of Anger in the Work of Love: Christian Ethics for Women and
Other Strangers," 3-21, and "Keeping Faith in a Sexist Church: Not for
Women Only," 206-34.

12. Daniel C. Maguire, in *The Moral Core of Judaism and Christianity:
Reclaiming the Revolution* (Minneapolis: Fortress Press, 1993), observes
that "Justice, indeed, is the primary love-language of the Bible. Jesus was
quite typical of his tradition in rarely speaking of 'love' " (128).

13. bell hooks, "Choosing the Margin as a Space of Radical Openness," in
Yearning: Race, Gender, and Cultural Politics (Boston: South End Press,
1990), 149.

14. Ibid., 149-50.

15. Suzanne Pharr recommends a visioning exercise for small workshop
groups, in which participants are asked, "What will the world be like without homophobia in it—for everyone, female and male, whatever sexual
identity?" As Pharr reports, "Just the imagining makes women alive with
excitement because it is a vision of freedom, often just glimpsed but
always known deep down as truth. Pure Joy." (Pharr, *Homophobia: A
Weapon of Sexism* [Inverness, Calif.: Chardon Press, 1988], 6, 8).

16. Larry L. Rasmussen, *Moral Fragments and Moral Community: A Proposal
for Church in Society* (Minneapolis: Fortress Press, 1993), 152-3.

17. Dorothee Soelle, *Revolutionary Patience*, trans. Rita and Robert Kimber
(Maryknoll, N.Y.: Orbis Books, 1977).

Index

American Psychiatric Association, 36
American Psychological Association, 36
Andolsen, Barbara, 10

battered women's movement, 23–24
battering, 99–100, 134–35 n. 11
Beirne, Piers, 95, 96, 134 nn. 6, 10
Bloomquist, Karen, 18–19, 56
bodily integrity, 82. *See also* body respect
body disrespect, 41. *See also* body wrong
body respect, 41, 82, 89–90
body wrong, 40–41. *See also* body disrespect; body respect
Briggs, Sheila, 30
Brown, Robert McAfee, 118
Brueggemann, Walter, 14, 69
Buber, Martin, 118
Bunch, Charlotte, 111–12

Christian ethics
  negative legacy regarding sexuality, 56–58, 59–62
  revitalizing of, 4–5, 77–78
  See also dominant sexual ethic; liberating sexual ethic; moral traditions, reconstruction of
Coffin, William Sloane, 23, 57
Collins, Patricia Hill, 45, 49, 52
Comstock, Gary, 68, 72.
control, 30–58, 94
Countryman, William, 87
crisis of sexuality

and absence of reliable moral tradition, 5–12
cultural context of, 15–17
See also sexual injustice dimensions of; sexuality

Davis, Angela, 48
D'Emilio, John, 47
disability, as moral failure, 40–44.
  See also sexuality
dominant sexual ethic
  assumptions of, 61–62
  a legacy of fear and control, 55–58
  See also Christian ethics
Douglas, Mary, 17–18

Eardley, Tony, 107
Ehrenreich, Barbara, 37
erotic power, 138 n. 11
  as moral resource, 8–9, 78–81, 106–7
  nexus of ethics and, 51–54
  and spirituality, 115–19
  See also eroticizing; justice
eroticizing
  of injustice, 1–2, 30–58, 76–77
  of justice, 76–93
  See also erotic power
ethics, nexus of eroticism and, 51–54. *See also* liberating sexual ethic; moral traditions, reconstruction of

Far from the Song of Songs, 129 n. 52. *See also* pornography
Farley, Margaret, 17

139

Index

Valverde, Mariana, 21, 31, 79,
violence, 26–27
    and masculinization, 102–7
    as a men's issue, 95–96
    a men's movement against, 96–102
    and men's silence, 107–12
    and military ideology, 102–5

Way, Peggy, 67
Weeks, Jeffrey, 18, 31–32, 34, 52

Weems, Renita, 72–73
Wendell, Susan, 42, 44
West, Cornel, 46, 48–49
Williams, Delores, 46, 125 n. 10

Yates, Wilson, 35
Young, Iris, 11

Zola, Irving Kenneth, 41–42

LaVergne, TN USA
14 October 2010

200758LV00005B/2/A